Hanzi Alive!

# 漢字有意思！

跟著劉墉一家趣味玩漢字

劉墉 Yung Liu —— 中文・圖

劉軒 Xuan Liu、劉倚帆 Yvonne Liu —— 英文

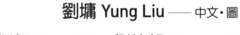

## ⊙ 引言 | Introduction

認識各體漢字，發掘文字起源，欣賞書法之
美，探尋趣味典故，學習中英語文，增添生活
樂趣，立即學以致用！

Learn Hanzi etymology, appreciate calligraphy
in its various forms, discover the origin of Chinese
characters and the stories behind them, and find
their use in daily life!

# ⊙ 目次 | Table of Contents

## ⊙ 每個字都像童話故事

Every word is an enchanted story

劉墉 Yung Liu

我女兒大學剛畢業就應聘去了北京，很多人驚訝她這個美國土生土長的女孩，有那麼好的中文程度，不但能聽能說能寫，甚至兩岸的繁簡體字和拼音、注音都會，猜我一定下了不少工夫教她。其實她小時候，我不過每週抽出一兩個小時給她上課，可能因為教法不同，所以能事半功倍。

My daughter landed her first job in Beijing straight out of college. People often remark how good her Chinese is, considering that she was born and raised in the U.S.. Not only is she fluent in both speaking and writing, but she is equally comfortable with traditional and simplified characters, and knows how to use the pinyin and zhuyin systems. Many think that this must have been the result of countless hours of toil and struggle, but actually it's been no more than one or two hours of lessons per week since she was a child.

由於我愛藝術、文學，又在美國的大學教「東亞美術概論」，所以我教漢字是從「文字學的藝術」入手。漢字由象形符號發展出來，本來就具有圖畫的性質，像是日、月、水、火、舟、車、蟲、魚，跟圖畫像極了，任何娃娃都一看就懂，何必讓孩子從起步，就認為文字是死板難學的呢？

Looking back, I believe the lessons are more efficient because I made character learning as fun as possible. Art and literature are my personal and professional passions, and I used to teach East Asian art studies in an American university, so I have always approached Chinese characters as an art form. Chinese Hanzi characters originated as pictographs, and still retain much of their pictorial past; words such as sun and moon, water and fire, boat and cart, insect and fish, are still just like pictures that can be readily explained to any young child. There is no reason why we should let children think these words are abstract and difficult to learn.

所以我用畫的，長長一條橫線，是地平線，加上圓圓的太陽，是太陽剛冒出地平線的「旦」；尖尖一個屋頂，裡面坐了個女生，是平平安安的「安」。媽媽帶著一個娃娃，多好啊！所以是「好」；一隻手在推，不夠！又來一隻手幫忙，是朋友的「友」……

For example, if you draw a horizontal line representing the horizon, and add a circle on top as a rising sun, what do you think it would mean? The resulting character「旦」means exactly what it looks like: dawn! Or if you draw a pointed rooftop, and add a character for woman (女) under it, the resulting character「安」means "safe." Put a woman and a child (子) together, and you get「好」, which means "good." One hand pushing is not enough; add a helping hand, and you get「友」, which means "friend." Modern words echo the values of the past.

由於文字經過長久地演變，現今使用的漢字，跟甲骨文和大小篆有很多不同。為了讓孩子能看出古人怎麼從觀察自然、創造文字，一步步演進到今天的樣子，我把真實的圖畫、刻寫的「甲骨文」、鑄造銘記的「金文」、秦代統一的「小篆」、方便記錄的「隸書」、文人獨特的「行草」和結構嚴謹的「楷書」，一個個排列起來。當孩子知道其中的變化，一方面會覺得有意思，一方面即使看到現今的繁體和簡體字，都能自然想到它們「當初的樣子」，那種追索的過程甚至有偵探和尋寶的趣味。

　　Still, having evolved through the centuries, a modern Chinese character can be markedly different from its original form. So, each word is presented first as a picture, then in its earliest written form on oracle bone shells, then as it was carved on early bronzeware, later as "small seal script" used in the Qin Dynasty, followed by "clerical script" developed for (obviously) clerical work, "cursive script" used by artists and literati, to the structurally balanced and complex "regular script." Arranged in sequence, it allows one to see how ancient Chinese people observed nature, created the words, and how it evolved through time. One can feel like an archeologist or a cryptographer, and knowing how the characters once looked thousands of years ago can certainly add to the appreciation of reading them today.

舉個例子，「采」這個字，上面是「手」，下面是「木」，手在樹上采，意思很明確，形象也簡單，只是後人在左邊又加了「一隻手」，成為後來的「採」。又譬如「本」字，中間直直一根樹幹，上面左右伸出兩根樹枝，下面伸出兩條樹根，在樹根的地方加一小劃，表示「根本」的道理。

　　As another example, the character「采」is a drawing of a hand on a plant, and later another "hand" was added on the left as a radical, forming the character「採」, which means "to pick".

　　If you draw a straight line as the trunk of a tree, horizontal lines as branches and slanting downward lines as roots, then add another small line near the base of the trunk, the resulting character「本」means "source" or "root".


　　為了讓寫實圖畫和文字符號的關聯更清楚，我除了畫圖，還用「剪影」。圖畫是彩色的，剪影是黑白的，前者比較複雜，後者比較簡化。譬如「犬」字，圖畫是一隻舉著前腳的狗，可能不容易和「犬」字聯想到一起，但是經過「剪影」，看來就有了緊密的關係。

　　To bridge the connection of written word and illustration even closer, I also depict the illustration as a silhouette; simplified into black and white, the pictures look more like the characters they became. For example, the character「犬」is of a dog lifting one front paw. As an illustration, it's not that obvious, but through the silhouette process, you can see much more readily how the picture becomes the word.

此外，文字是實用的，孩子愈能用在生活中愈好。所以在我教漢字的時候，只要遇到有中文的場合，無論街上的招牌或餐館的菜單，立刻會指著字讓孩子認。我兒子原本不懂簡體漢字，跟我去大陸一個月，一路上看招牌認字，就學得差不多了。

Of course, the written word is a tool, and beginning learners should make use of it in daily life as much as possible for it to stick. Back when I taught my children, I would have them identify characters whenever we see them, whether it's on a street sign or a restaurant menu. My son couldn't read simplified Chinese at first, but after a month long trip through Mainland China, he was able to learn it by reading all the signs.

所以我又用了一種方法，就是四處拍照，要孩子從照片裡找他認識的字。因為漢字全球化，我拍照的地點除了臺灣、中國大陸、香港，也包括日本、泰國、馬來西亞和新加坡等這些跟漢字關係密切的地方。我發現每個孩子都天生愛尋寶，當他才學幾個字，就能從生活照片裡找到，會特別興奮，也記得特別牢。

So in this book, I also use this method to teach character recognition, by taking photographs of Chinese characters throughout the world. In my experience, every child and beginning learner loves to hunt for the words they just learned in photographs and surroundings. Even if they only know a few characters, it's very exciting for them to spot these words in life, and it certainly enhances their memory.

加上今天是個國際化的社會，最好讓孩子從起步的時候就能雙語溝通，我在教漢字的時候也以英文解釋，又為了讓孩子印象深刻，甚至讓他有成就感，每次都要孩子把我寫的中文翻譯成英文，而且放在這本書裡。所以這本書應該既適合西方人學中文，也可以作為中國孩子的英語教材。

Society in the future is ever more global, so I believe it's best to develop proficiency in more than one language as early as possible. When teaching Chinese to my children and my students, I sometimes use English to explain. My children now are the ones who did the English translation for this book. I believe it can be a useful tool not only for English readers wishing to learn Chinese, but can work the other way around as well.

更進一步，雖然今天十三億人都用簡體漢字，而且簡體字比繁體字好寫得多，但繁體字是我們偉大的文化資產，就算筆劃多，不易寫，也應該懂。所以我在教孩子的時候是繁體、簡體，甚至「注音」、「拼音」一起進行的。

In addition, I believe in learning both the traditional and simplified characters together, and I have taught my children to use both the pinyin and zhuyin phonetic systems. Although simplified characters are the norm for the majority of Chinese, the traditional (also known as "complex") script is a cultural heritage in itself. They may have many more strokes and take longer to write, but it's still worthwhile to study and appreciate them.

或許正因為從「圖像」、「剪影」、「符號」，到文字演進一路教下來，非但能加深印象，收事半功倍的效果，孩子也在自然間感受書法的美。我相信如果每個人都能從漢字源頭上學起，以後認字的方法和趣味會大大不同，文字不再只是死板的符號，而是生動的圖畫或故事。

　　In this sequence of learning a word through pictures, silhouettes, symbols to text, I believe that the impression will be deeper, and learners can naturally begin to appreciate the beauty of calligraphy as well. I truly believe that if everyone can learn Chinese characters by studying their source, the written language itself will come alive.

　　這本書的各體漢字和插圖都是我繪製的，我原本可以從字典或電腦檔案裡直接取用文字，但為了親自體會漢字的美，還是一筆一劃地臨寫，由於書寫的時間不同，或許有好有壞，請大家諒解。

　　All of the illustrations and calligraphy in this book were done by yours truly. I could have sampled from reference books or computer fonts, but still decided to write them by hand, so the reader can more fully feel their organic beauty. Since they were done over different periods of time, their quality may be slightly different, and I apologize for their imperfection.

至於英文，如前面所說是由我女兒邊學邊譯，當年她還小，英文能力有限，所幸這是寫給小朋友的書，英文太深奧反而不好，所以雖然後來經過劉軒校正，仍然盡力保持原樣。

The English translation of the text was first done by my daughter. At the time of the first draft, she was still quite young, and her prose not so polished, but as this is a book meant for beginning learners and children, I thought it best to keep the language simple. My son later did some editing, but mostly kept the translations as they were.

這本書雖然不大，前後卻花了多年時間，直到女兒上大學才停止。至於出版更因為需要補足考證，我的教學工作又忙，結果一拖再拖，差點半途而廢。所幸而今孫子女到了認字的年齡，逼我重拾舊業、野人獻曝，把我教學的心得與大家分享。我不是專業的文字學家，同一個字也可能有各家不同的解釋，闕誤之處在所難免，請大家不吝指教！

This book is not big, but has been a long time coming. I worked on it as a family project, all the way until my daughter left for college. In the meantime I kept busy with other things, and some of the material had to be more fully researched, causing further delays that almost stalled the project completely. Luckily, my grandchildren are now at the age to learn Chinese characters for the first time, which motivated me to pick up where I left off, and I now humbly present this work to you. I sincerely welcome your comments, and hope that learners of Chinese everywhere, young and old, may enjoy and benefit from this book!

# ⊙ 這本書的使用方法

How to use this book

這本書是透過圖畫、剪影和各種字體介紹漢字的演進。

This book introduces the etymology of Chinese Hanzi characters through illustrations, cutouts and various written forms of a character throughout history.

它能改變你看漢字的態度，讓學寫字不再是刻板的功課而是生動的藝術，讓每個漢字不再只是符號，而成為看圖說故事。

Learning Chinese characters in this way becomes less of a chore and more like art. A character is no longer a symbol but an illustrated story.

更有趣的是，在每個漢字之後都有一張在世界各地拍攝的照片，讓你像是尋寶般在裡面找出剛學的那個字，使文字立刻跟你的生活結合。

In addition, each character is accompanied by photographs taken from around the world. You can search for the character in its environment, thus making a connection between the character and what you see in daily life.

請看下面的例圖：

For example:

# HOW TO use THIS BOOK

第一頁

這一頁是個楷體字和它的注音,同時附加了中國大陸使用的拼音。你可以先打開這一頁,猜猜這是什麼字?

Page 1:

The introduction to each character opens with a page of the character in regular complex script, together with its phonetic spelling in zhuyin and pinyin forms. You can use this page as a flashcard to test yourself in the future.

第二頁

這一頁的上方是以生動的彩色圖畫,表現字的源頭,下方是很淺白易懂的中英文解說。

Page 2:

This is a color illustration showing the pictographic meaning of the character, followed by a simple explanation.

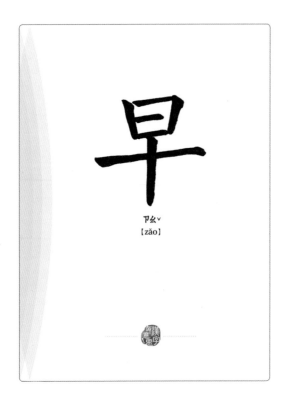

ㄗㄠˇ
[zǎo]

「早」!中國人早上一見面總說「早」,意思是「早安」。
「早」這個字意思是太陽剛升出草地。「早」也可以用來形容「提前」和「前面的時間」,像是「早起早睡」、「早期」、「早年」。

「早」 is what the Chinese say when they see greet each other in the morning. What they mean is "good morning."

The character 「早」 represents the sun just rising from the grass. 「早」 can also be used as a modifier meaning "in advance" or "preceding period of time" in expressions such as 「早起早睡」 (early rise, early sleep), 「早期」 (early period), and 「早年」 (early years).

14 漢字有意思!
Hanzi Alive!

第三頁

這一頁的上方是與第二頁相對應的剪影，它可以讓大家很自然地把圖畫和文字聯想在一起。下方從左到右介紹那個文字從甲骨文、大篆、小篆、隸書、行書到楷書的演變。（317到331頁還有各種字體的中英文解說。）

第四頁

一張彩色照片，拍自臺灣、中國大陸、香港、星馬、日本、或其他與中文有關的地方。新教的字藏在一堆招牌或風景裡，請讀者小心地找出那個字。這樣做的目的是既有尋寶的趣味，又能讓大家把剛學的字帶到生活當中，養成很好的學習態度：在生活中學習！學習用在生活！

Page 3:

Top of this page is the illustration from page 2 transformed into a silhouette. This acts as a visual "bridge" between the illustration and the written forms of the character. On the bottom of the page, from left to right, shows the character's evolution through history, from oracle bone script to regular script. An extended introduction to the various script forms can be found on pages 317-331.

Page 4:

Here is a photograph taken from various locations where Chinese characters can be seen. The character you have just learned will be somewhere in the photograph. By looking for it like an Easter egg hunt, you can link the word with its naturally appearing context. Learning from daily life and putting that into use is certainly the best attitude to have when learning Chinese characters!

# ⊙ 漢字有意思！

Hanzi Alive !

一

【yī】

　　「一」是最簡單的中文字。查中文字典時，「一」總在第一個。「一」是數字，又因為它是最前面的數字，所以有最初的意思；「一」還表示只有這麼一個，是獨一無二的，所以也形容「獨家的」、「統一的」。譬如「一家之言」，「一天下」，意思是「獨創的言論」和「統一天下」。

　　「一」更因為樣子像地平線，所以跟別的符號合用，可以表示很多意思。

　　「一」, meaning "one," is the most basic Chinese character. In Chinese dictionaries, 「一」 is always the first character presented. 「一」 is a number, and because it is the first number, it also means "the first." 「一」 can also mean "the only one" (獨一無二) as well as "unique" (獨家的) or "united" (統一的). 「一」 is also readily combined with other parts to build characters with different meanings, as we shall see.

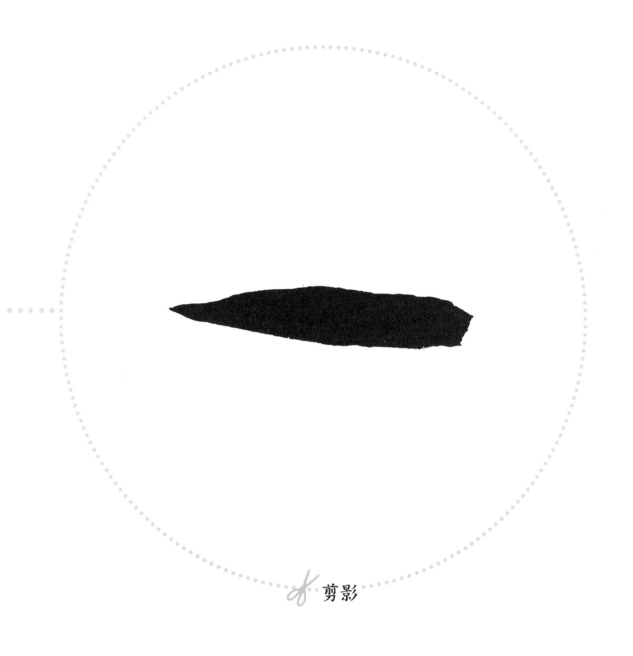

剪影

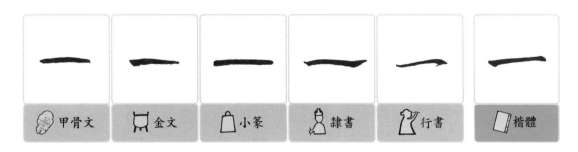

甲骨文　　金文　　小篆　　隸書　　行書　　楷體

一起找一找

一：攝於香港。

ㄕㄤˋ

【shàng】

　　「上」是現在中文的寫法，右頁中間兩個是很早以前在甲骨文和銅器上的寫法。意思是在地平線的上面。大概為了避免與「二」這個數字混淆，後來漸漸發展為用三筆寫成的「上」。

This is 「上」, meaning "up" or "above." The second and third characters on the down of the opposite page are the way 「上」 was inscribed on oracle bones ／ tortoise shells and bronzewares. The written form eventually evolved into 「上」 with three strokes, perhaps because people did not want it to be confused with 「二」 which is the number "two".

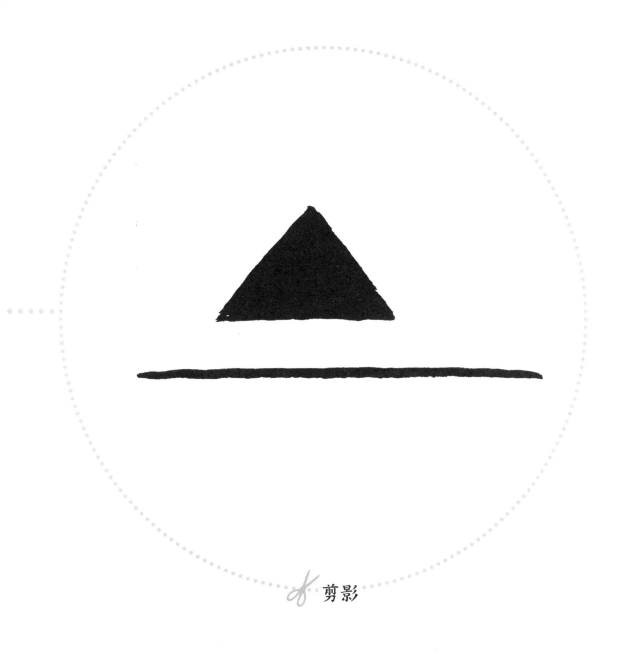

剪影

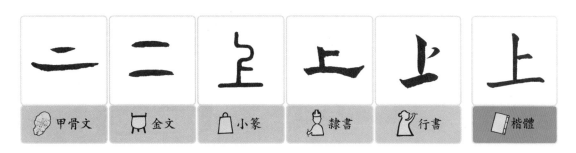

| 甲骨文 | 金文 | 小篆 | 隸書 | 行書 | 楷體 |

ㄒㄧㄚˋ

【xià】

知道了「上」，一看這個字，就曉得它的意思是「下」了。

After knowing the meaning of 「上」, you can probably see how 「下」
means "down" or "under."

漢字有意思！
Hanzi Alive!

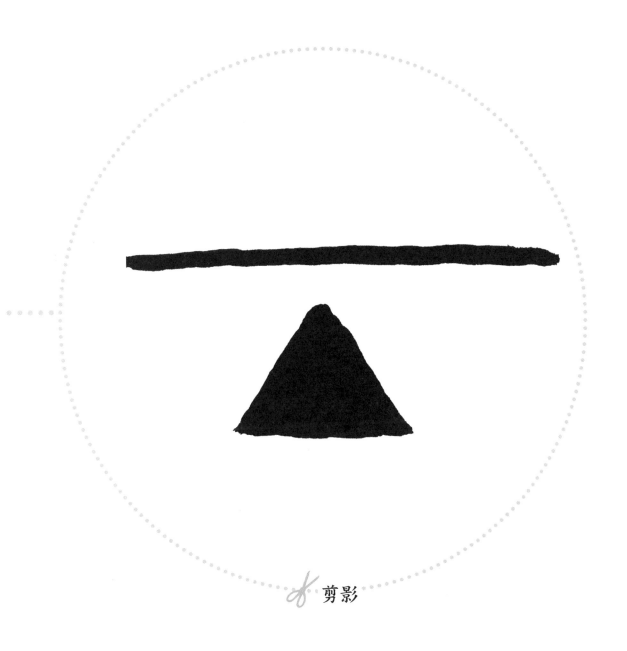

剪影

| 甲骨文 | 金文 | 小篆 | 隸書 | 行書 | 楷體 |

使用後敬請順便將
盥洗枱抹擦乾淨以
方便下一位旅客使用

As A Courtesy To The Next Passenger
May We Suggest That You Use Your
Towel To Wipe Off Wash Basin

日、

【rì】

「日」是象形文字，本來寫成如右邊「☉」的樣子。有人認為中間的一個黑點，表現古人看太陽時見到的「太陽黑子」。

「日」, meaning "sun" or "day," is a pictograph. It was written as 「☉」in ancient times. Some believe that the dot in the middle represents sunspots.

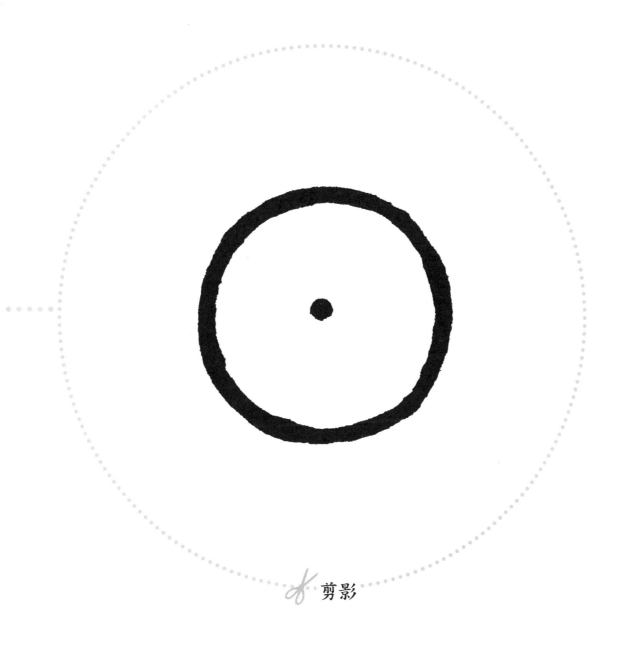

剪影

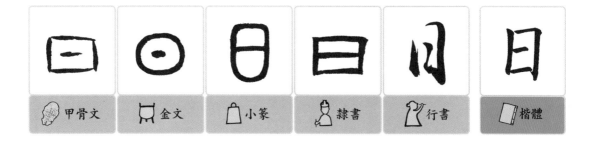

| 甲骨文 | 金文 | 小篆 | 隸書 | 行書 | 楷體 |

一起找一找

日：攝於北京。

ㄉㄢˋ
【dàn】

太陽出現在地平線上，意思是天剛亮的時候。

When the sun rises above the horizon, it forms 「旦」, meaning "dawn."

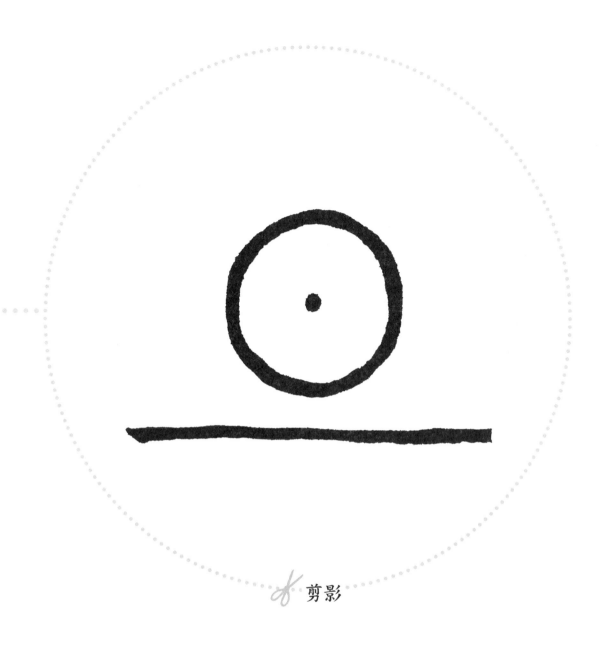

剪影

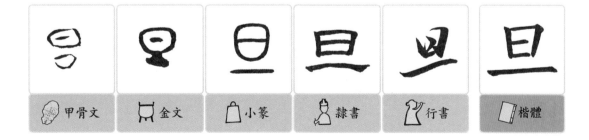

| 甲骨文 | 金文 | 小篆 | 隸書 | 行書 | 楷體 |

ㄗㄠˇ

【zǎo】

「早」！中國人早上一見面總說「早」，意思是「早安」。

「早」這個字表現的是太陽剛升出草地。「早」也可以用來形容「提前」和「前面的時間」，像是「早起早睡」、「早期」、「早年」。

「早」is what the Chinese say when they see greet each other in the morning. What they mean is "good morning."

The character「早」depicts the sun just rising from the grass.「早」can also be used as a modifier meaning "in advance" or "preceding period of time" in expressions such as「早起早睡」(early rise, early sleep),「早期」(early period), and「早年」(early years).

剪影

| 甲骨文 | 金文 | 小篆 | 隸書 | 行書 | 楷體 |

一起找一找
早：攝於臺北。

ㄩㄝˋ

【yuè】

　　看右邊的五種不同時期的寫法，可以知道，月這個字是怎麼由一彎新月變成的。它原本是畫天上彎彎的月亮，又在月亮上加了一些「月影」，漸漸成為今天的寫法。

「月」, is the word meaning "moon" or "month." Take a look at how it was written through five different time periods. You can see how 「月」 evolved from the shape of a new moon to a moon with some shadow, then gradually into the way it is written nowadays.

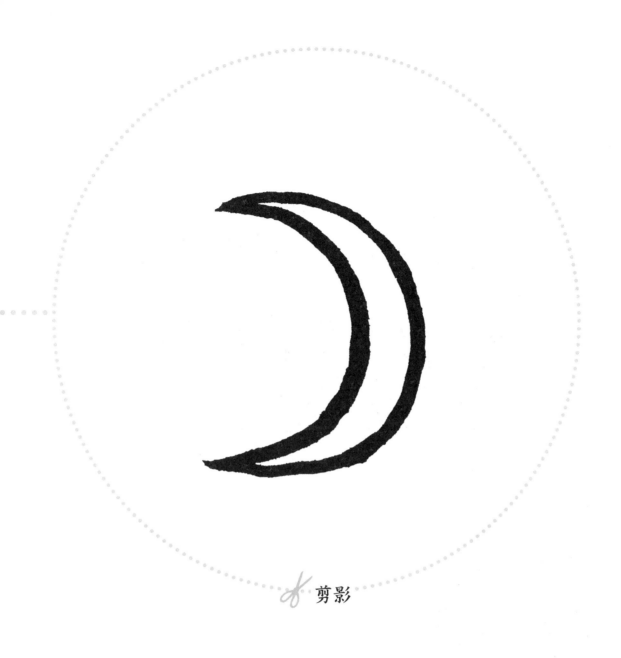

剪影

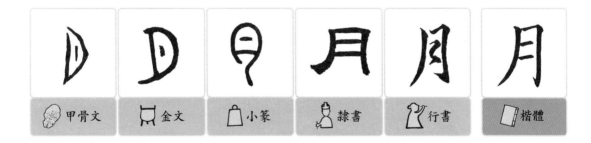

| | | | | | |
|---|---|---|---|---|---|
| 甲骨文 | 金文 | 小篆 | 隸書 | 行書 | 楷體 |

# 明

ㄇㄧㄥˊ

【míng】

　　如果有一天，天上同時出現太陽和月亮，一定會特別怎樣？當然特別明亮！

　　這個「明」字也有另一種說法：左邊是窗子，右邊是一彎明月，明月照進窗子，很明亮。

If there were a day when both the sun and the moon appeared at the same time, it would be especially "bright," which is the meaning for「明」.

Another explanation of this character is that the left side is a window, and the moon shines through the window, making things "bright."

剪影

甲骨文　金文　小篆　隸書　行書　楷體

一起找一找

明：攝於雲南。

ㄊㄧㄢˊ

【tián】

　　幾千年前中國人的田,跟現在看起來差不多,有種莊稼的田地,還有中間交叉和四周圍繞的田埂。

This is the character for "farm." Chinese-style farms thousands of years ago did not look much different from the ones of today. Ridges intersect and surround the plot of land used for planting.

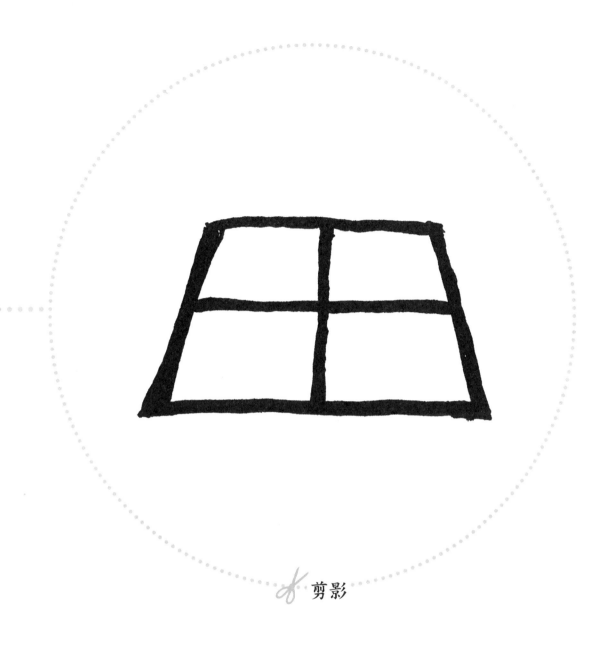

剪影

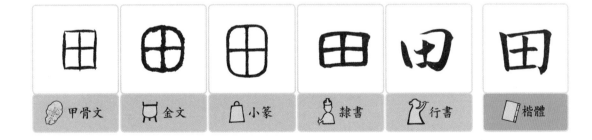

| 甲骨文 | 金文 | 小篆 | 隸書 | 行書 | 楷體 |

一起找一找

田：攝於臺北剝皮寮。

ㄋㄢˊ

【nán】

　　如果你是到中國旅行的外國人，一定要認得「女」和「男」這兩個字。「男」很好認，尤其甲骨文，像用犁去耕田，在田地裡努力工作的就是「男」。現在的「男」字是「田」加「力」。如果不記得，只要認得上方格子的田就成了。

If you are visiting China, you must know the two words: 「女」(female) and 「男」(male). 「男」is quite easy to recognize, especially by its oracle bone inscription, which looks like a man farming with a plow. The modern character is a combination of 「田」(farm) and 「力」(strength). Just remember the rectangle on the top, and you can recognize it at a glance.

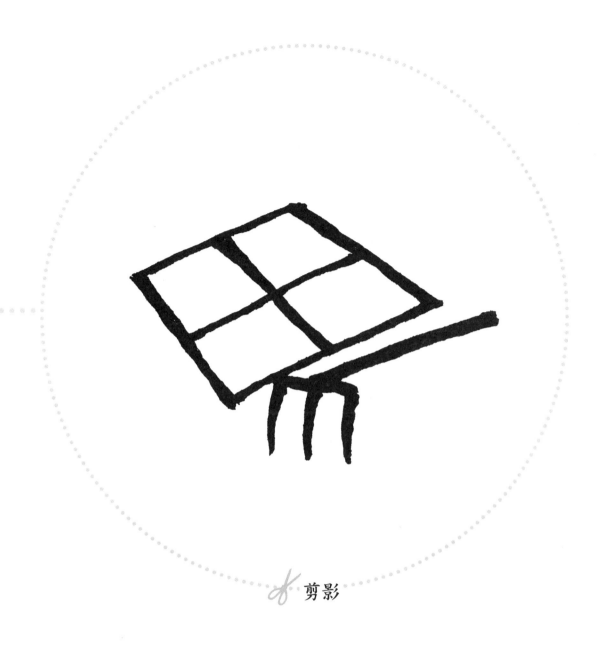

剪影

| 甲骨文 | 金文 | 小篆 | 隸書 | 行書 | 楷體 |

# 男 一起找一找

男：攝於臺北禪園（張學良故居）。

ㄋㄩˇ

【nǔ】

一個人半蹲半坐，伸手向前，在膝上交叉，這是個很安閒的「女」人。

「女」, meaning "woman" or "female," depicts a person half sitting and half kneeling, with her hands folded on her knees in a relaxed pose.

剪影

| 甲骨文 | 金文 | 小篆 | 隸書 | 行書 | 楷體 |

一起找一找
女：攝於香港。

ㄏㄠˇ

【hǎo】

　　這是中國人最常用的「好」字，左邊一個女人，右邊一個娃娃：女人帶孩子，好極了！女人生孩子，好極了！女人揹娃娃，好極了！你學中文，別的字可以不學，先要學這個「好」字。你與人見面，可以說「好」；你同意，可以說「好」。

This is the most frequently used word「好」, meaning "good." The left side of「好」is a woman; the right is a baby. A woman with a baby, how wonderful! A woman having a child: great! A woman carrying a child on her back: excellent!

If you learn only one Chinese character, let it be「好」. When you greet people, say「好」for "hello." When you agree , say「好」for "yes."

剪影

| 甲骨文 | 金文 | 小篆 | 隸書 | 行書 | 楷體 |
|---|---|---|---|---|---|

ㄢ

【ān】

女人待在屋子裡，很平安！這就是「安」。

把「安」與「早」一起用，是「早安」。把「安」和「好」一起用，是「安好」。把「安」和「日」一起用，是「日安」。

A woman in a house: peaceful. This is「安」.

「安」can be combined with different words to form different phrases:

「早」+「安」=「早安」"good morning"

「安」+「好」=「安好」"safe and sound"

「日」+「安」=「日安」"good day"

剪影

| 甲骨文 | 金文 | 小篆 | 隸書 | 行書 | 楷體 |

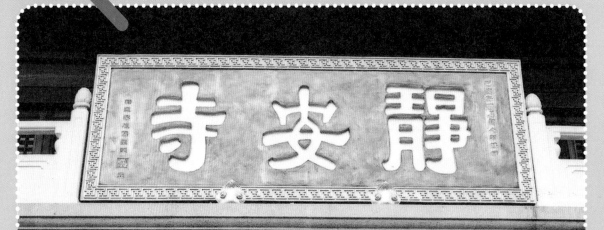

ㄖㄣˊ

【rén】

　　介紹完女人，當然要介紹男人，這個「人」字，可以指所有的人類，也可以專指男人，它是由象形文字發展出來的，看來好像一個站著的人的側面。

After introducing "women," we will now learn words relating to men. The frequently used character「人」means "a man," but it also applies universally to all genders.「人」developed from a pictograph showing the profile of a standing person.

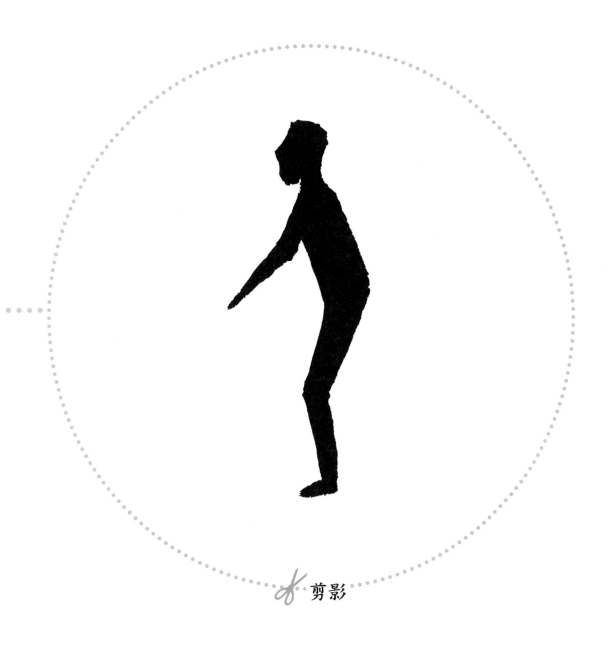

剪影

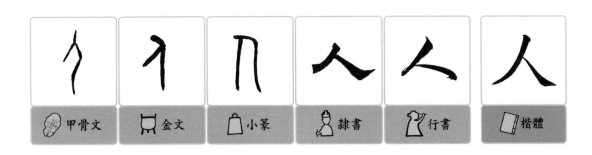

| 甲骨文 | 金文 | 小篆 | 隸書 | 行書 | 楷體 |

一起找一找

人：攝於昆明花博園。

ㄒㄧㄠˇ

【xiǎo】

最早甲骨文的「小」，只是三個小點子，意思是一點點。後來發展成中間一條直線，左右各一個小點子。有人認為直線表示切開，把大的切成小的。

The original inscription of「小」was three small dots, meaning "a little bit." Afterwards, it developed into one straight line in the middle with a dot on each side. Some people believe that the line represents cutting something into small pieces.

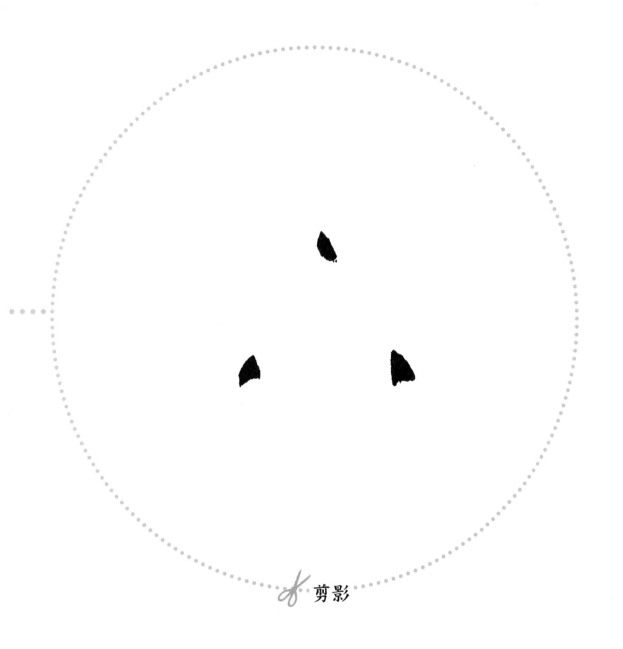

剪影

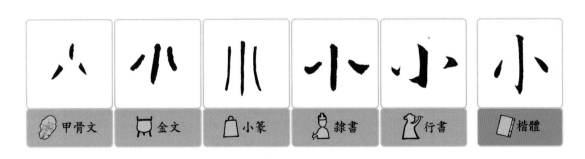

| 甲骨文 | 金文 | 小篆 | 隸書 | 行書 | 楷體 |
|---|---|---|---|---|---|

# Little India

## 小 印 度

## லிட்டில் இந்தியா

 North East Line NE

| Destination | First train | | | Last train |
|---|---|---|---|---|
| | Mon-Fri | Sat | Sunday & Public Holiday | Daily |
| to NE1 HarbourFront | 6.02am | 6.02am | 6.23am | 11.4 |
| to NE17 Punggol | 6.10am | 6.10am | 6.30am | 12.05am |

ㄉㄚˋ

【dà】

一個把兩臂和雙腿伸開的人，很健壯的樣子，是「大」。

This character shows a person standing with arms and legs outstretched, making himself look "big," which is what this characters means.

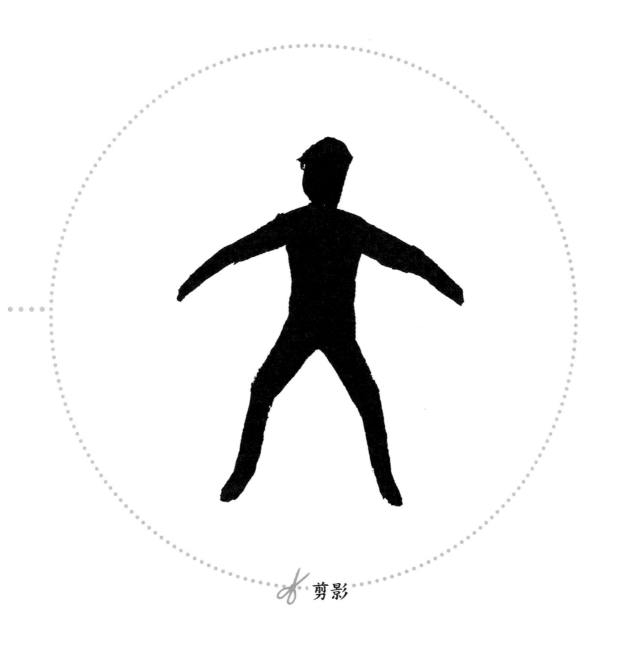

剪影

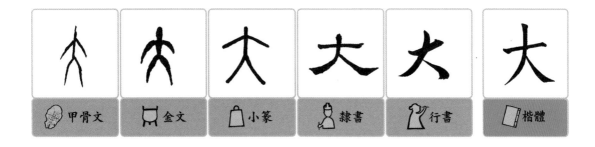

甲骨文　金文　小篆　隸書　行書　楷體

大

一起找一找

大：攝於上海。

ㄈㄨ

【fū】

　　古時候，成年的男人都要戴帽子，這個象形字就是「夫」。「夫」指大男人，也指「丈夫」。「夫人」是「丈夫的人」，就是太太。

　　「夫」 is a pictograph showing a man wearing a hat, and it means "a grownman," and also means "husband."

　　「夫人」("the person with husband") is a polite way of addressing someone's wife.

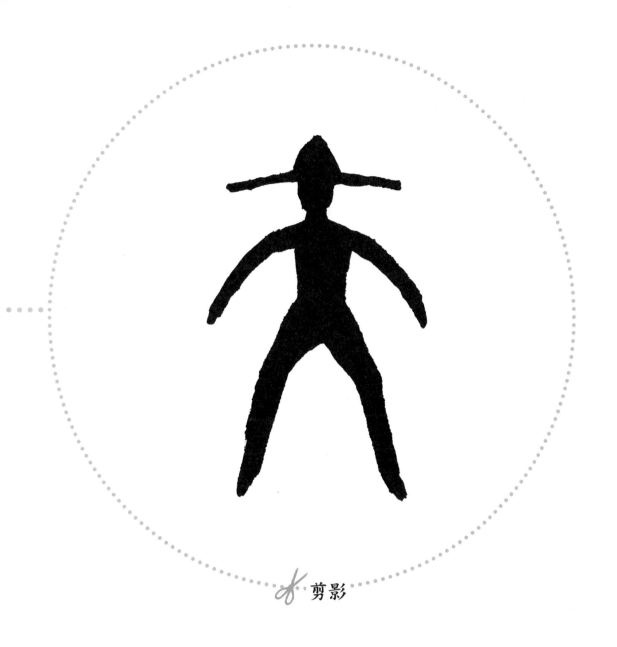

剪影

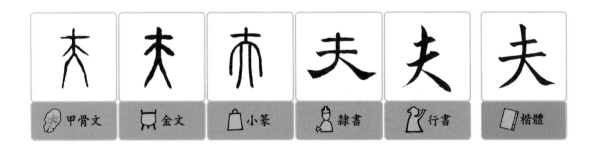

| 甲骨文 | 金文 | 小篆 | 隸書 | 行書 | 楷體 |

ㄊㄧㄢ

【tiān】

　　如果在「大」上面畫一橫，就表示人們頭頂上的「天」。

　　把前面學過的「好」和「天」放在一起，是「好天」，意思是好的天氣。把天和「好」字右邊的「子」放在一起，是「天子」，意思是「天的孩子」，也就是「皇帝」。

Drawing a line on top of 「大」 represents the sky, forming 「天」.

Put 「好」 and 「天」 together forms the phrase 「好天」, meaning "good weather." Put 「天」 and 「子」 together forms 「天子」(literally, "the son of heaven"), which is another title for the Emperor of China.

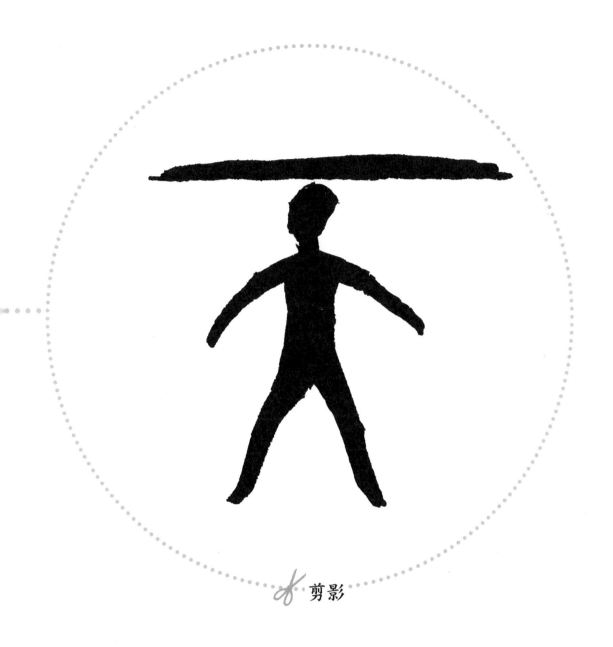

剪影

| 甲骨文 | 金文 | 小篆 | 隸書 | 行書 | 楷體 |

ㄐㄧㄠ

【jiāo】

　　一個站著的人，兩腿交叉，是「交」。交有交叉、交換、交錯的意思，譬如「交友」、「交心」、「交通」。

A person standing with his legs crossed is「交」.
「交」means "intersect," "exchange," or "crisscross." For example,
「交友」means "making friends" (think of "crossing paths with");
「交心」means "heart-to-heart"; and「交通」means "traffic."

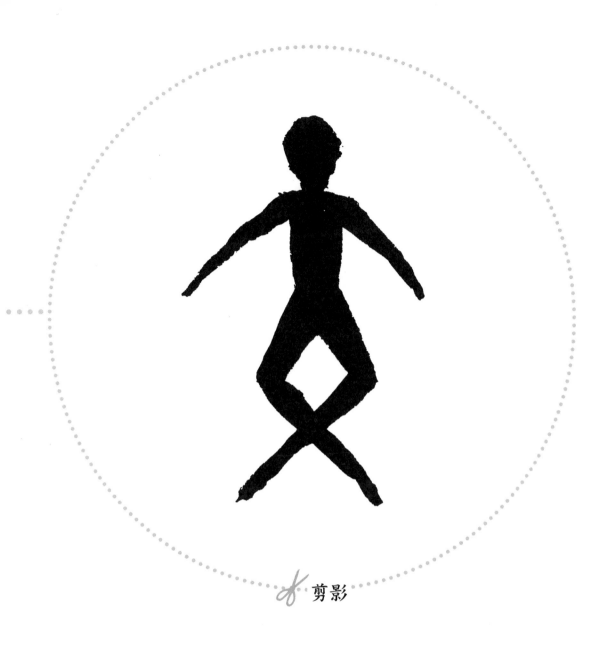

剪影

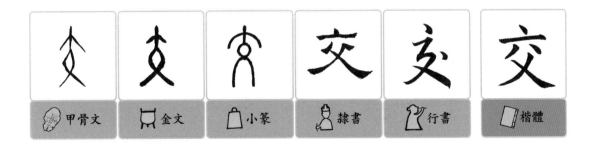

| 甲骨文 | 金文 | 小篆 | 隸書 | 行書 | 楷體 |

交通銀行
BANK OF COMMUNICATIONS

# 保管箱

营业时间：9:00－18:30
星期六　日不休息

营业时间
上午9:00－下午5:00
（星期六、日休息）
储蓄时间
9:00－18:30
星期六、日不休息

ㄌㄧˋ

【lì】

　　這個字一看就像個正面站著的人，下面一橫，表示地面，意思是一個站在地上的人。中國人常說「三十而立」，表示三十歲的人要自己站著，不能再讓父母操心了。

This character looks like what it means: a person standing upright. The horizontal line at the bottom of the character represents the ground. A popular Chinese saying「三十而立」means that by the age of 30, a man should be able to stand up and support himself without any help from his parents.

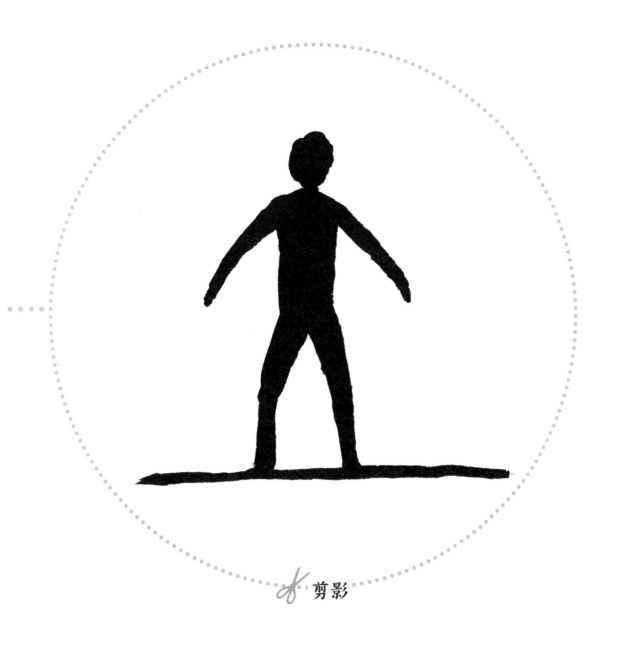

剪影

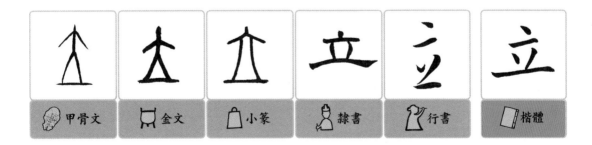

| 甲骨文 | 金文 | 小篆 | 隸書 | 行書 | 楷體 |

アヌˇ

【shǒu】

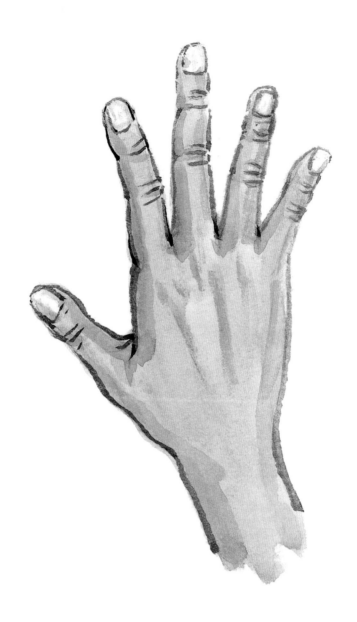

「手」是象形字，看來就像五根手指。後來慢慢發展成兩種寫法：
「扌」是用作偏旁時的寫法；「手」是單獨指「手」的時候的寫法。

　　「手」is a pictograph that looks like five fingers of a hand. The character developed into two written forms:「扌」is used as a radical to form other characters, while「手」is used by itself to mean "hand."

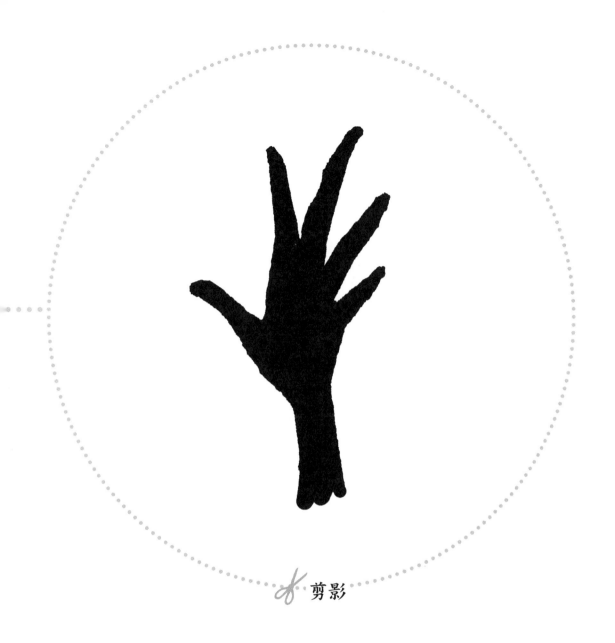

剪影

| 甲骨文 | 金文 | 小篆 | 隸書 | 行書 | 楷體 |

metro Taipei

請家長留意小孩
的手勿靠在門上
避免夾傷。
To avoid injury, keep
children's hands clear
of the doors.

小心夾手
Mind your hands!

ㄧㄡˇ

【yǒu】

　　手也能簡化成「ㄢ」，兩隻手朝同一個方向，表示一隻手在工作，另外一隻手過去幫忙，就是朋友的「友」。

「手」can also be written in a simplified form as「ㄢ」. Two hands in the same direction expresses the idea of one hand working and another hand helping. This becomes the character「友」meaning quite fittingly as "friend."

剪影

| 甲骨文 | 金文 | 小篆 | 隸書 | 行書 | 楷體 |

ㄕㄡˋ

【shòu】

下面一隻手，把一個盤子似的東西從上面一隻手上接過來，是「受」。

A hand at the bottom taking a plate-like object from a hand on top is「受」, meaning "to receive."

剪影

甲骨文　金文　小篆　隸書　行書　楷體

ㄞˋ

【ài】

如果「受」的盤子裡放著一顆心，就是「愛」。

If you take「受」, and put a heart on the platter, it becomes「愛」, which means "love." Offering one's heart on a platter, is a poetic description of love indeed!

剪影

| 甲骨文 | 金文 | 小篆 | 隸書 | 行書 | 楷體 |
|---|---|---|---|---|---|

# 一起找一找

愛：攝於沖繩。

ㄈㄢˇ

【fǎn】

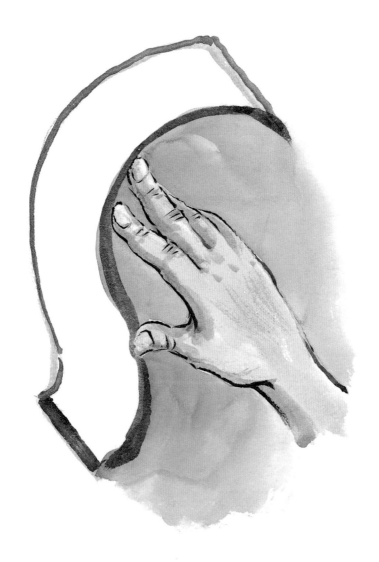

　　在一隻手的前面，畫一個波浪似的線，表示用手把東西翻過來，意思是「反」。東西上下左右或正反面顛倒是「反」，不服從可以說「反」。不同意和抗拒也是「反」。

Drawing a wavy line in front of a hand implies the hand is turning something over, which is「反」. When something is in an opposite direction, whether up-down, left-right, or in-out, it is referred to as「反」.「反」can also mean "to disobey," "to disagree," or "to go against."

剪影

| 甲骨文 | 金文 | 小篆 | 隸書 | 行書 | 楷體 |

ㄇㄨˋ

【mù】

　　「木」是象形字，中間一直，是樹幹；樹幹上方是樹枝，下方朝著地的是樹根。

　　「木」, meaning "tree" or "wood," is another pictograph. The vertical line down the center represents the tree trunk, while the horizontal line on the top are branches and the two slanting lines at the bottom are the roots.

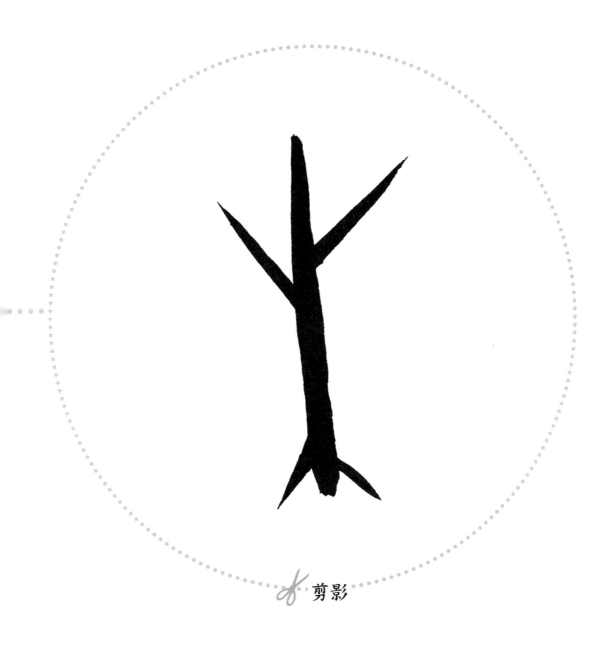

剪影

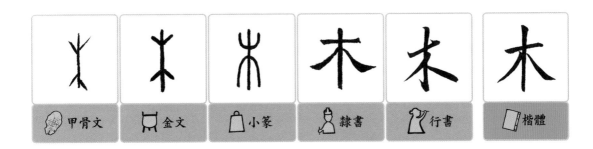

| 甲骨文 | 金文 | 小篆 | 隸書 | 行書 | 楷體 |

一起找一找

木：攝於臺北建國花市。

ㄅㄣˇ

【běn】

如果在根的位置，加一小劃，表示專門指樹根。

根本！「本」就是「根」。

前面我們學過了「日」，如果把「日」和「本」放在一起，就成為「日本」這個國家的名稱。他們為什麼自稱「日本」？因為他們認為自己的國家是太陽的根，太陽是由那裡升起的。

A short line drawn to mark out where the roots are in 「木」 makes the character 「本」. 「本」 means "roots" or "origin."

Remember the character 「日」 from the beginning of the book? Combining 「日」 and 「本」 makes 「日本」, which means "Japan." Why would the Japanese name their country as 「日本」? For they believe that they are the land where the sun rises.

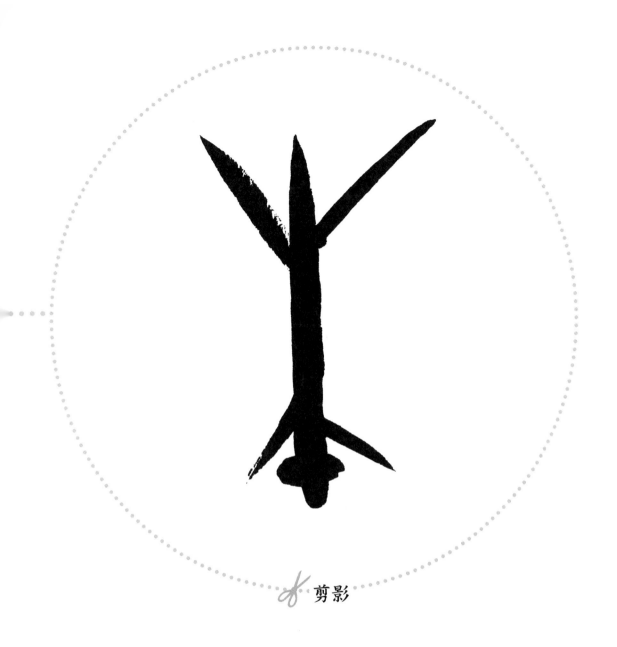

剪影

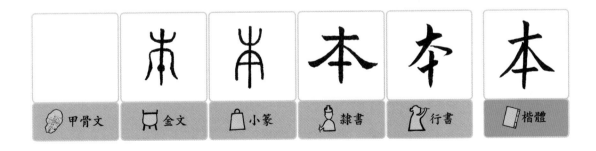

| | | | | | |
|---|---|---|---|---|---|
| 甲骨文 | 金文 | 小篆 | 隸書 | 行書 | 楷體 |

ㄌㄧㄣˊ

【lín】

兩個「木」，表示樹很多，是「林」。

Two 「木」 make 「林」, which represents many trees or "the woods."

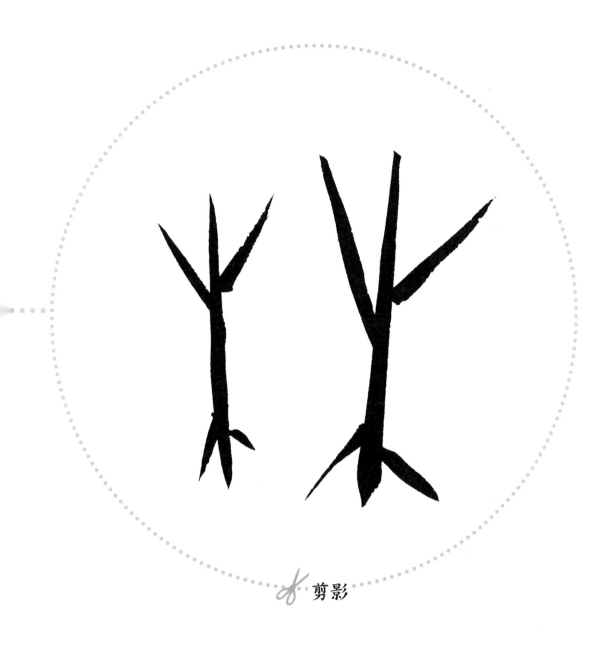

剪影

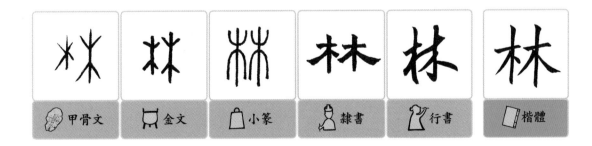

一起找一找

林：攝於雲南石林。

ㄙㄣ

【sēn】

　　如果把三個「木」寫在一起，表示樹更多了，是「森」，中國人常把「森」和「林」合用，成為「森林」。

Three「木」, three trees, make a forest with even more trees than「林」.「森」also means "forest." In fact, the Chinese often use「森」and「林」together as「森林」to mean "forest."

剪影

| | | | | | |
|---|---|---|---|---|---|
| 甲骨文 | 金文 | 小篆 | 隸書 | 行書 | 楷體 |

大安森林公園
Daan Park

2號出入口
No.2 Entrance & Exit

ㄘㄞˇ

【cǎi】

　　一棵樹上有三個果子，從上面伸出一隻手，做什麼？採花！採果子！這個字就是「采」。採後來變得比較複雜，在左邊多加了一隻手，成為用兩隻手採。

A tree has three fruits, with a hand on top picking the fruits. This character 「采」 means "to pick." This character later became slightly more complex, adding another hand to help with the picking.

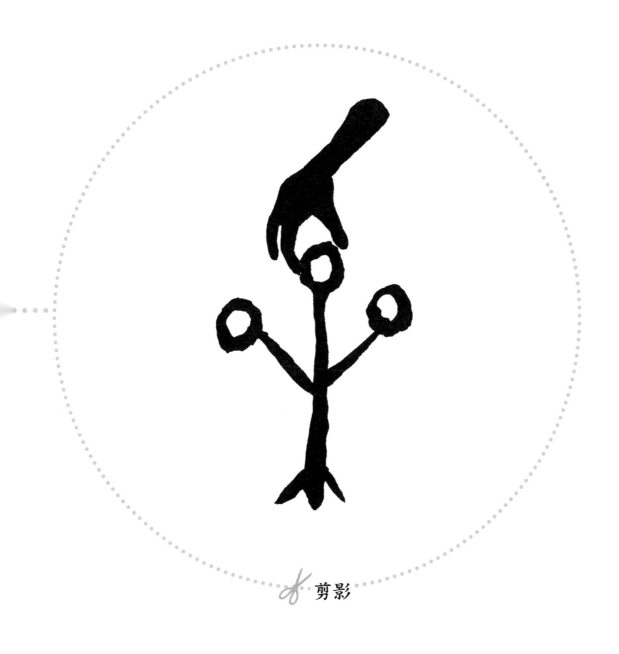

剪影

| 甲骨文 | 金文 | 小篆 | 隸書 | 行書 | 楷體 |

ㄉㄨㄛˇ

【duǒ】

　　木的樹枝上，彎彎地伸出一朵花，這個象形字就是「朵」，中國人用朵作為花的量詞，譬如「三朵花」，就是三個花。

The curves of a flower growing out of a tree is the pictograph「朵」.「朵」is used as a unit-measuring word for flowers. For example, "three flowers" would be written as「三朵花」.

剪影

| | | 籴 | 柔 | 柔 | 朵 |
|---|---|---|---|---|---|
| 甲骨文 | 金文 | 小篆 | 隸書 | 行書 | 楷體 |

ㄓㄨˊ

【zhú】

「竹」是象形字，就像是每組三片，共六片的竹葉。

「竹」 is a pictograph. It resembles bamboo with two sets of three leaves.

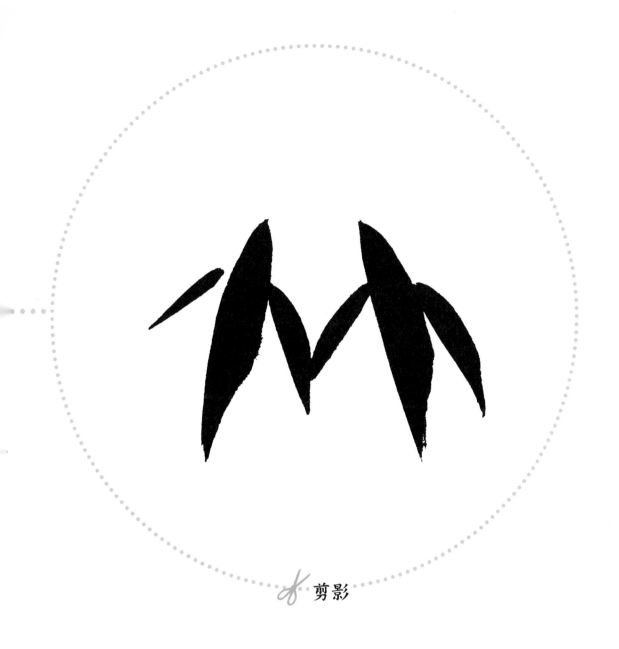

剪影

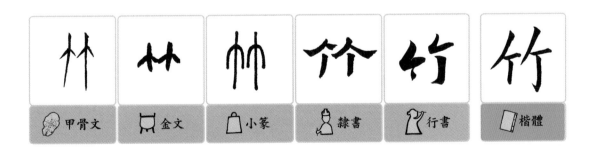

甲骨文　金文　小篆　隸書　行書　楷體

ㄅㄧˇ

【bǐ】

五根手指拿著一根用竹子做的尖尖的東西，那根東西是什麼？是「筆」！

Five fingers holding a pointed object made of bamboo – what is that object? It is「筆」, meaning"pen."

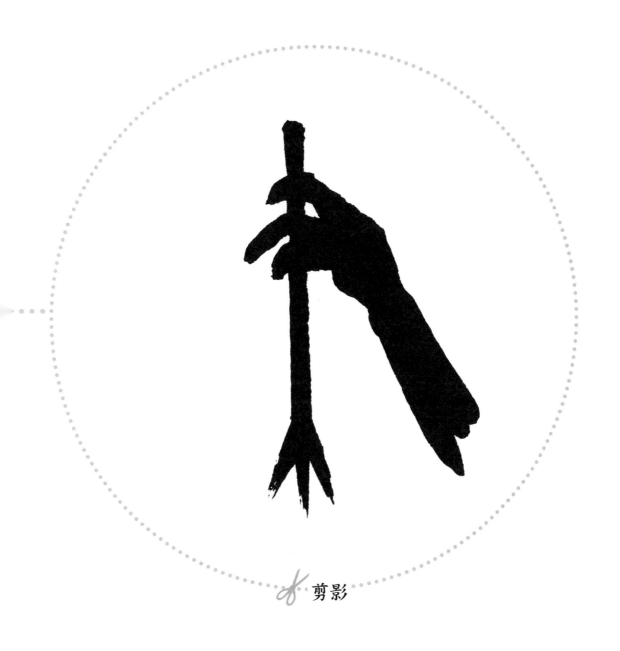

剪影

| 甲骨文 | 金文 | 小篆 | 隸書 | 行書 | 楷體 |

筆

一起找一找

筆：攝於山西太原。

書

ㄕㄨ

【shū】

　　「書」起初不是名詞，而是動詞，也就是拿著筆寫字。看看！中間垂直的是筆，上面是不是有五根手指？下面的「日」表示寫出的東西。

The original character for「書」was not a noun, but a verb that means "to write with a pen." Look! The straight line down the middle is a pen, and do you see five fingers holding it? The「日」down below is what was written by using the pen.

漢字有意思！
Hanzi Alive!

剪影

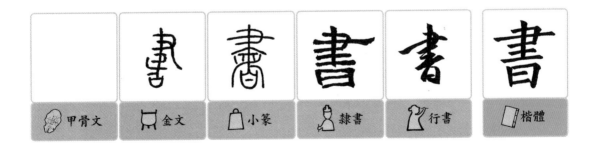

| | | | | | |
|---|---|---|---|---|---|
| | 畫 | 書 | 書 | 書 | 書 |
| 甲骨文 | 金文 | 小篆 | 隸書 | 行書 | 楷體 |

一起找一找

書：攝於廣州。

ㄏㄨㄚˋ

【huà】

　　由前面介紹的「筆」字可以知道「聿」是五指握筆。如果下面再加「皿」，表示在東西上畫了圖，就是「畫」。

　　「畫」是動詞，也是名詞，譬如「畫畫」，前面是動詞，後面是名詞。

We have already introduced「筆」, which means "pen." The「聿」under the bamboo in「筆」depicts a hand holding a pen. If we add「皿」under it, it shows that we have drawn something. That is「畫」meaning "to draw" or "to paint."

　　「畫」can be used both as a verb and a noun. In「畫畫」, the first「畫」character functions as the verb "to paint" and the second「畫」as the noun "painting." Together they mean "to paint a painting."

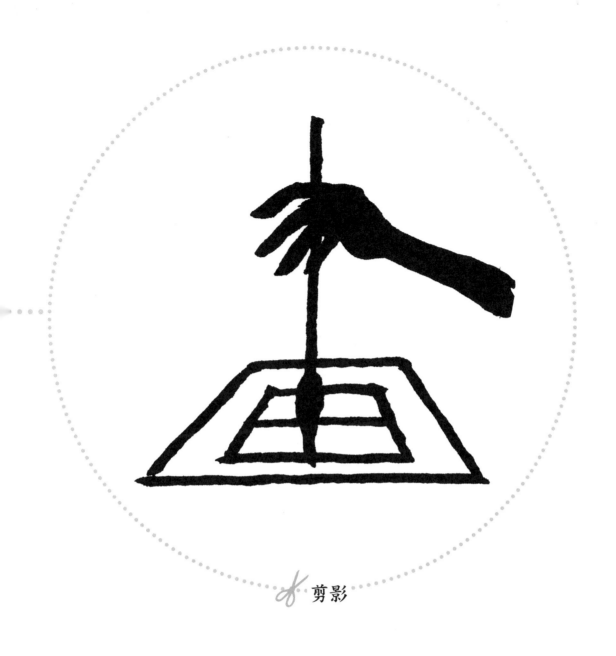

剪影

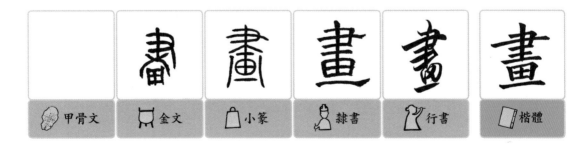

| 甲骨文 | 金文 | 小篆 | 隸書 | 行書 | 楷體 |

ㄎㄡˇ

【kǒu】

這個看來像一張笑嘻嘻的嘴的字，是「口」。中國人管一個人叫一口。

This character, which looks like a smiling mouth, means just that: "mouth." The Chinese sometimes refer to mouths as a unit to count people, eg. one person =「一口」.

剪影

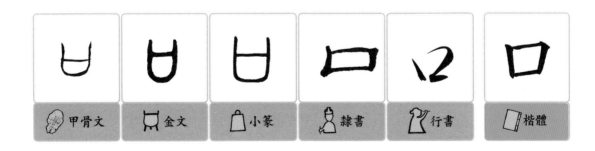

| 甲骨文 | 金文 | 小篆 | 隸書 | 行書 | 楷體 |

ㄇㄧㄥˊ

【míng】

　　上面一彎月，下面一個口，意思是在月光不亮的晚上，人們彼此看不清，於是告訴相遇的人：「我是誰，叫什麼名字」。這個字就是「名」。

This character is formed by a new moon on top and a mouth at bottom. Think of a moon-lit night, when people cannot see each other clearly, and must call out their names to let others know who they are. Therefore, "name" (or title) is the meaning of this character.

剪影

| 甲骨文 | 金文 | 小篆 | 隸書 | 行書 | 楷體 |

一起找一找

名：攝於臺北龍山寺。

彳

【chī】

這個字太重要了！左邊一個口，右邊好像食物的香氣或蒸氣，意思是「吃」。如果食物很美味，則在前面加個「好」，說：「好吃！」

This word is extremely important! There is a mouth on the left, and on the right is what appears to be steam or the delicious smell of food. The meaning of this character「吃」is "to eat." If the food is good, one can simply add「好」before the「吃」, to say「好吃」: "good eat"= delicious!

剪影

| 甲骨文 | 金文 | 小篆 | 隸書 | 行書 | 楷體 |
|--------|------|------|------|------|------|
|  |  | 吃 | 吃 | 吃 | 吃 |

一起找一找
吃：攝於臺北。

# 門

ㄇㄣˊ

【mén】

「門」，一看就知道是個象形字，好像兩扇半開的門。

「門」，meaning "door," looks just like a set of double doors.

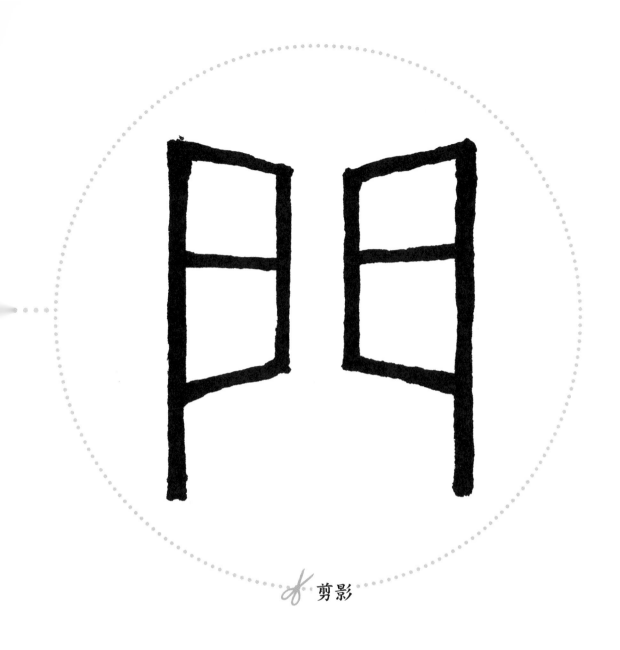

剪影

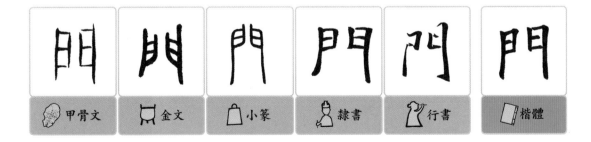

| 甲骨文 | 金文 | 小篆 | 隸書 | 行書 | 楷體 |

一起找一找

門：攝於日本。

ㄨㄣˋ

【wèn】

把門拉開一點，在中間放一張嘴，是「問」，好像有人在門外問話。

A mouth placed in between opening doors symbolizes someone outside the door is asking a question;「問」means "to ask."

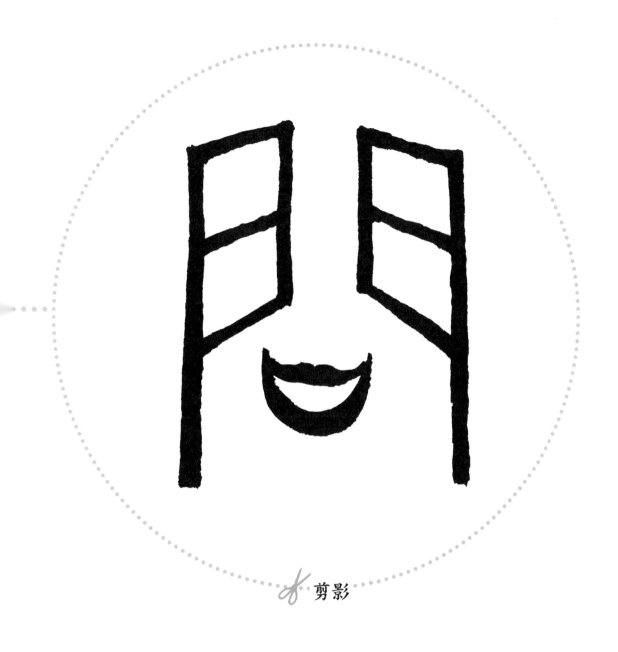

剪影

甲骨文　金文　小篆　隸書　行書　楷體

# 問 一起找一找

問：攝於臺北。

閒

ㄒㄧㄢˊ

【xián】

沒人來問，門半掩著，中間看見一彎月，多悠閒哪！這個字正是「閒」。

The door is half-open with no one outside to bother you, and a crescent moon can be seen through open doors. This character「閒」means "idle"or "unoccupied."

剪影

| 甲骨文 | 金文 | 小篆 | 隸書 | 行書 | 楷體 |

儿ˇ

【ěr】

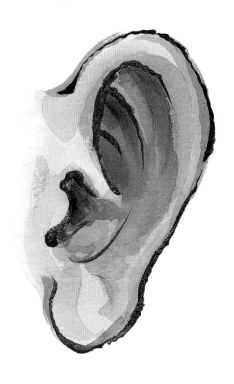

耳是象形字，就像一隻耳朵。

「耳」is a pictograph: it looks like an ear, which is what it means!

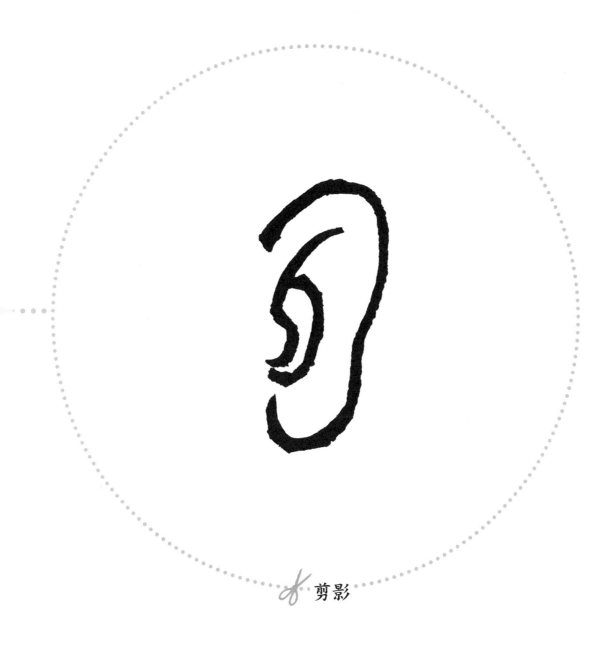

剪影

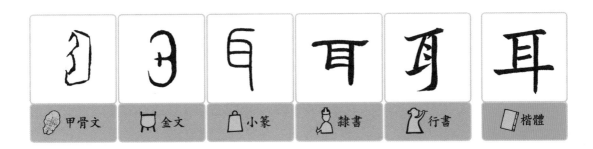

| 甲骨文 | 金文 | 小篆 | 隸書 | 行書 | 楷體 |

ㄇㄨˋ

【mù】

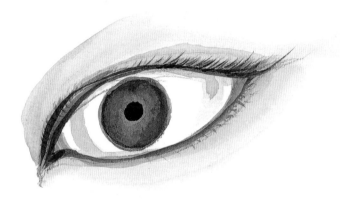

目的象形字，一看就知道像隻眼睛，但是後來為了方便跟別的字拼在一起，漸漸把「」打直了，成為現在「目」的寫法。

The pictograph「」looks obviously like its meaning: an eye. But in order to be combined with other characters, it was rotated sideways to become its present form「目」.

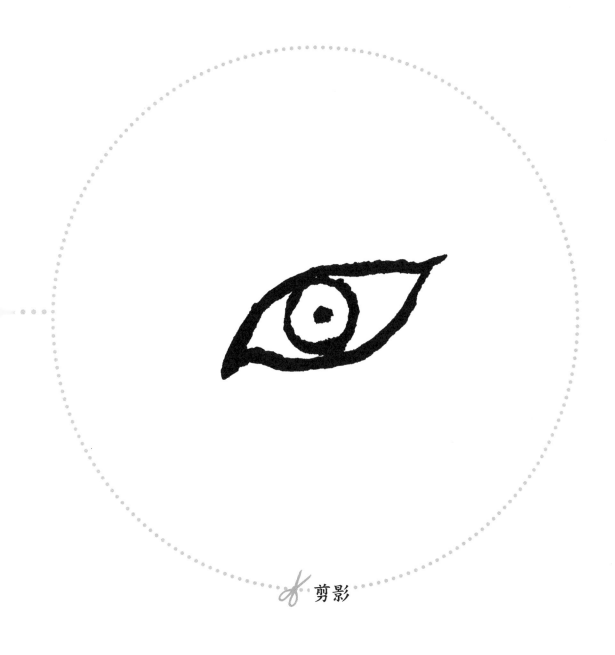

剪影

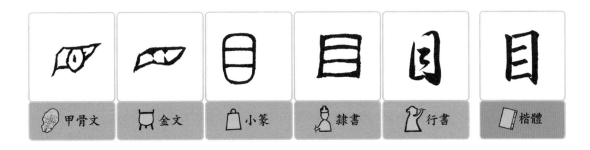

| 甲骨文 | 金文 | 小篆 | 隸書 | 行書 | 楷體 |

ㄎㄢˋ

【kàn】

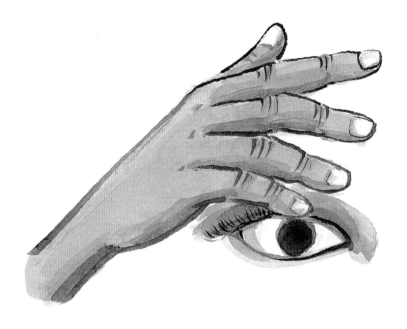

太陽大，看不清，於是用手遮著眼睛，這是「看」。

The sun is bright and it's hard to see, so one raises a hand to shield the eyes.
This is the character「看」, meaning "to see."

剪影

| 甲骨文 | 金文 | 小篆 | 隸書 | 行書 | 楷體 |

一起找一找

看：攝於貴州。

...的腹胀、腹痛

...石、结石性胆囊炎

...管、肝内胆管结石

...膀胱、尿道结石

...尿管绞痛

内有厕所

B超为什么只能作参考

明明白白看病
明码标价.收费...

ㄐㄧㄢˋ

【jiàn】

　　一個身體，上面頂著一隻大大的眼睛是「見到」的「見」。

　　「看」和「見」不一樣，「看」比較是「現在式」；「見」常常是「完成式」。中國人常說「看見」，意思是「看了！而且見到了！」

A body with a big eye on top is 「見」, meaning "to see." However, 「見」 is different from 「看」 in that 「看」 is the act of seeing in the present tense, while 「見」 describes a past act of seeing. When the Chinese say 「看見」, the complete meaning is "I see, and I saw!"

剪影

| 甲骨文 | 金文 | 小篆 | 隸書 | 行書 | 楷體 |

ㄅㄧˊ

【bí】

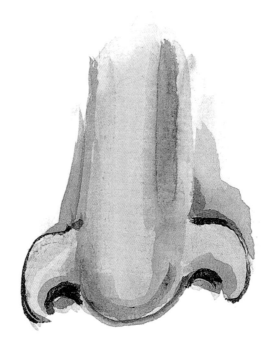

「鼻」字是象形字，看來像是一個鼻子，鼻孔正在呼吸。

「鼻」, "nose" is another pictograph which looks like a nose with nostrils breathing.

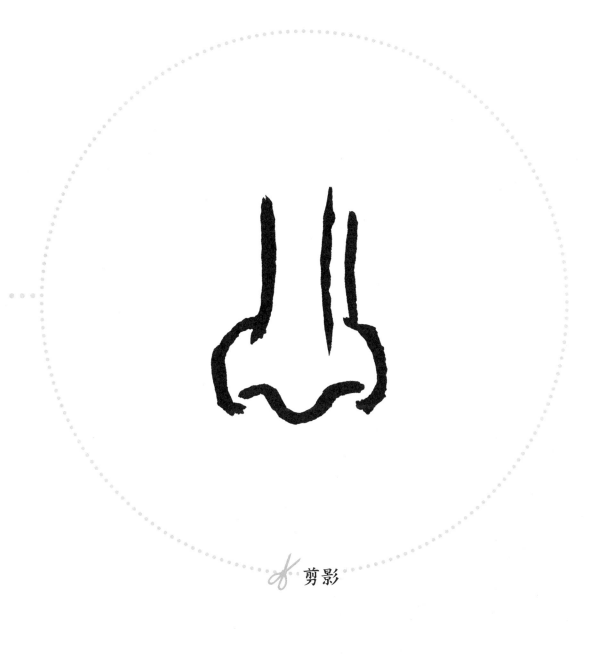

剪影

| 甲骨文 | 金文 | 小篆 | 隸書 | 行書 | 楷體 |

ㄖㄡˋ

【ròu】

「肉」最早的寫法跟「月」有些相似，像是吊掛著的一塊肉。

The earliest form of this character 「肉」looks very similar to 「月」, but what it depicts is a hanging piece of meat.

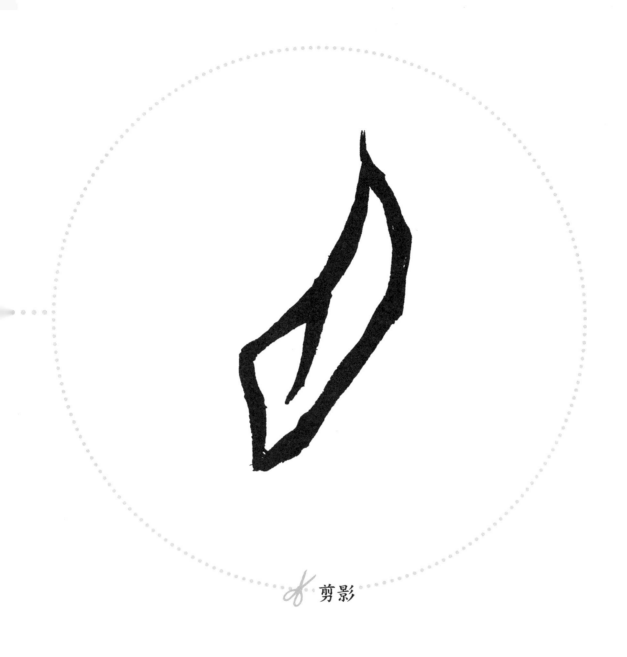

剪影

| | | | | | |
|---|---|---|---|---|---|
| 甲骨文 | 金文 | 小篆 | 隸書 | 行書 | 楷體 |

ㄗˇ

【zǐ】

　　在介紹「好」字的時候，談到過「子」，就像一個用布包著的娃娃。用布包著嬰兒身體，既不會著涼，娃娃又覺得好像被人緊緊抱著，有安全感。

　　When we learned 「好」 previously, we were also introduced to 「子」, meaning "baby." Indeed, the character looks like a baby wrapped in a blanket. The baby in the blanket will not catch cold; she will also feel safe and loved.

剪影

甲骨文　金文　小篆　隸書　行書　楷體

八仙圖

親事乙巳

平佛夏业

月仿介乎圍

為卒

銀同陳氏

第一等人忠臣與孝子

ㄩㄣˋ

【yùn】

一個大肚子的女人，肚子裡有個娃娃，她懷「孕」了！

A woman has a big belly. In her belly, there is a baby. She is "pregnant" which is the meaning of this character.

剪影

| 甲骨文 | 金文 | 小篆 | 隸書 | 行書 | 楷體 |

婦產科提供所有婦女完整的連續性
從新婚健康檢查、不孕症中心、優
到一般產科、婦科服務…等
我們用高品質的服務
一路關心並伴隨您的健康

財團法人
基督復臨
安息日會
Adventist
HOSPITAL

臺安醫院

女人．初為人

新婚健康檢查

．諮詢分機 2581

ㄗˋ

【zì】

在屋子裡誕生了一個娃娃，是「字」。最早的意思是生孩子，現在變成文字的「字」。你也可以想是一個小孩在屋子裡學寫字。

A baby is born in a house; it is 「字」. The character's earliest meaning was "to give birth," but now it means "a word." You can also think of it as a child learning how to write words in a house.

剪影

| | 甲骨文 | 金文 | 小篆 | 隸書 | 行書 | 楷體 |

ㄖㄨˇ

【rǔ】

　　孩子餓了，於是由媽媽抱在懷裡哺乳，最左邊的象形字是甲骨文上的，活像一個摟著娃娃的媽媽。只是後來把媽媽的「身體」和「手」分開了，成為今天的「乳」字。

The baby is hungry, so the mother feeds the baby with her breast. The leftmost oracle bone pictograph looks like a mother holding a baby in her arms. In later era, the mother's body and hands were separated, becoming today's「乳」, meaning "breast" or "milk."

剪影

甲骨文　金文　小篆　隸書　行書　楷體

ㄕㄢ

【shān】

　　甲骨文的「山」就像三座連在一起的山。演變到現在也差不多，橫的一筆是地平線，垂直的三筆是高高的山峰。

The oracle bone inscription for「山」looked like a mountain range with three peaks, and it has not changed much since then. The modern character shows a horizontal line for the horizon and three vertical lines for the peaks.

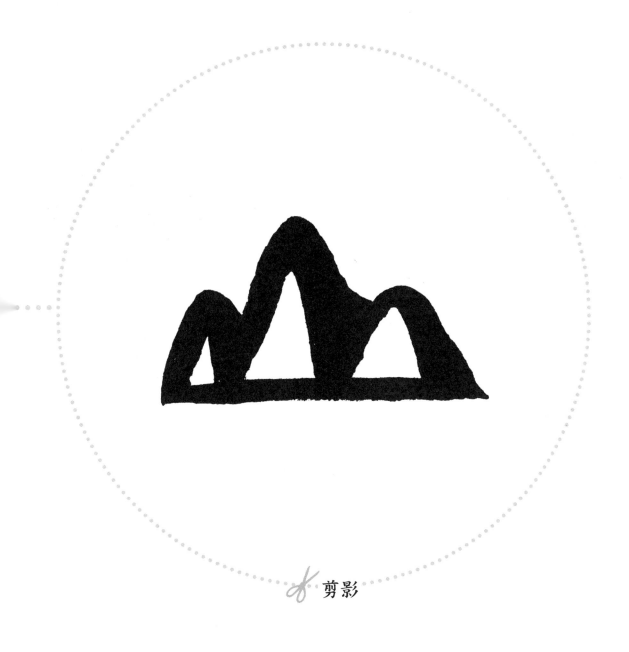

剪影

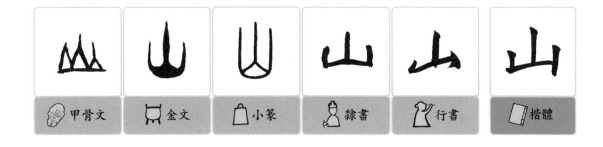

| 甲骨文 | 金文 | 小篆 | 隸書 | 行書 | 楷體 |

## 一起找一找

山：攝於馬來西亞檳城。

ㄕㄨㄟˇ

【shuǐ】

這個象形字，一看就像流動的水，也好像由高處看到的一條河。所以在中文字裡，「水」可以指水這個流體，也可以指河流。

This pictograph looks like moving water, or like a river viewed from above. Thus, the word「水」can mean both "water" and "river."

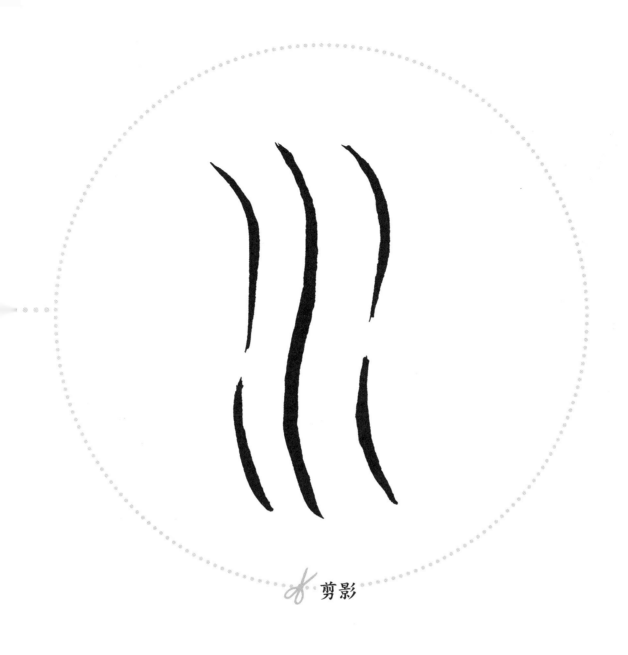

剪影

甲骨文　金文　小篆　隸書　行書　楷體

一起找一找
......................
水：攝於香港。

ム

【sī】

　　「絲」的象形字，一看就知道是兩縷絲線。許多跟連接有關的字，都用「絲」作邊，但為了好寫，只用半個「絲」，也就是「糸」。

The original pictograph for this character looks like two bundles of silk. 「絲」means "silk" but may also refer to other types of threadlike things. Just as a silky thread is continuous, many words related to "connecting" also have 「絲」as part of the word. But to make the character easier to write, only one half of 「絲」, or 「糸」is used.

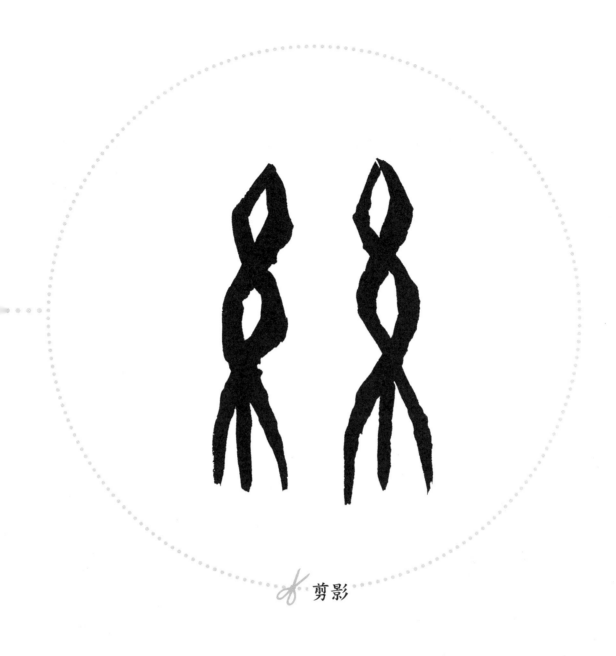

剪影

| 甲骨文 | 金文 | 小篆 | 隸書 | 行書 | 楷體 |

歡迎光臨 WELCOME

工廠直營

純綠豆

火鍋粉絲

銷經總 北區
靠可用信

福州油麵

一ㄡˋ

【yòu】

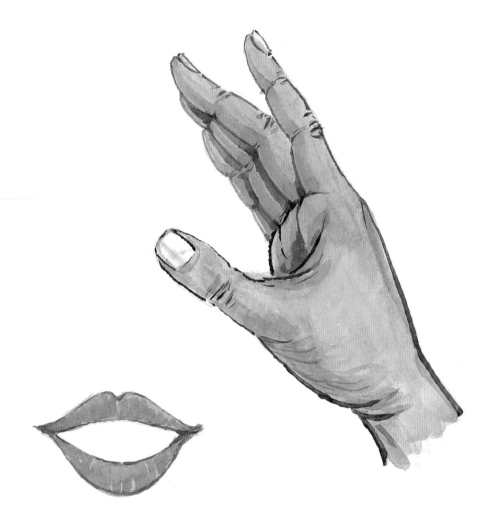

　　最初甲骨文的「右」，只畫一隻右手。後來為避免跟「手」這個字搞混，加了「口」，專指左右方向的右。當然也可能表示一邊以右手做事，一邊說話。

The first inscription of「右」was simply the image of a right hand.「口」was later added for clarity. It may also mean that people often work with the right hand while talking at the same time.

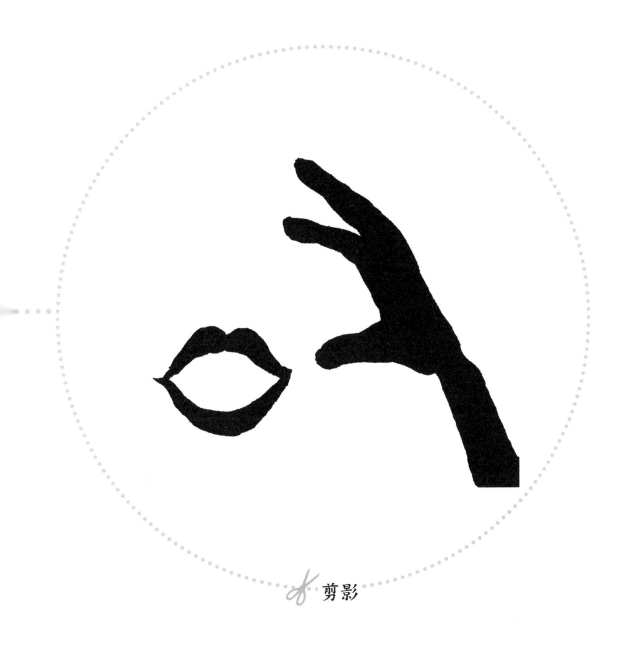

剪影

甲骨文　金文　小篆　隸書　行書　楷體

ㄗㄨㄛˇ

【zuǒ】

　　最初甲骨文的「左」，只是畫個左手，後來加上「工」，意思是左手拿工具。那工具很可能是尺，因為人們常用左手拿尺，右手作記號，所以拿尺的是左手。

The earliest inscription of「左」showed only the image of a left hand. The「工」later added represents a tool being held by the left hand. That tool was most likely a ruler, because people often hold the ruler with their left hand, while they mark or draw with their right hand.

剪影

甲骨文　金文　小篆　隸書　行書　楷體

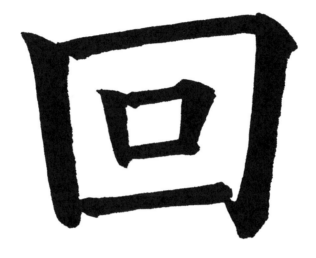

ㄏㄨㄟˊ

【huí】

　　「回」這個字很常用，譬如「回家」、「回來」。它有往回轉的意思，
是由「一條彎曲迴轉的河流」象形字發展出來。

　　「回」is a frequently used word, in such phrases as「回家」(return home)
and「回來」(come back). The character evolved from the picture of a river
bend.「回」means "to circle" or "to return."

剪影

甲骨文　金文　小篆　隸書　行書　楷體

ㄕㄥ

【shēng】

　　在地面上長出一株草，是「生」，意思是生長、出生、誕生、生育，從無到有。

A few blades of grass growing from the ground becomes「生」, which means "to be born," "to grow," "to live," or "getting something where there was nothing before."

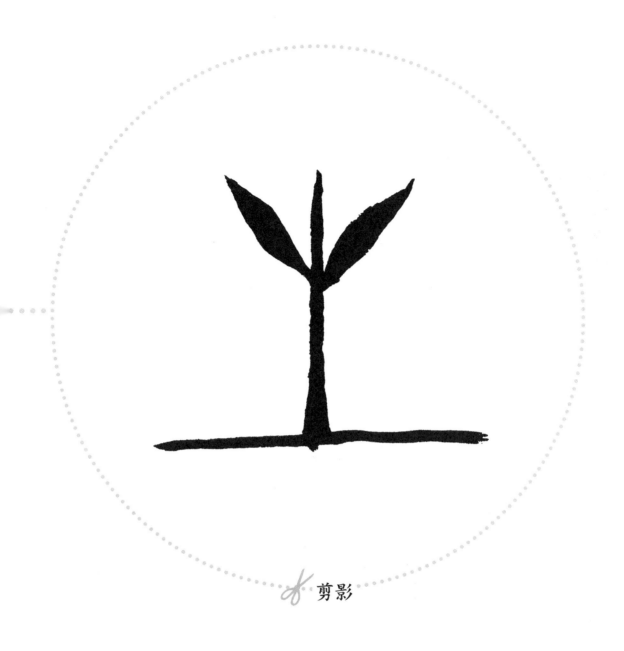

剪影

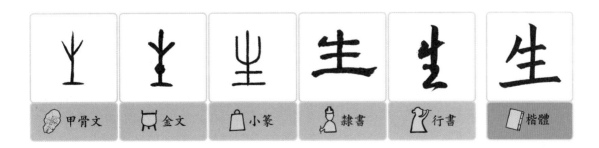

| 甲骨文 | 金文 | 小篆 | 隸書 | 行書 | 楷體 |

## 一起找一找

生：攝於臺北。

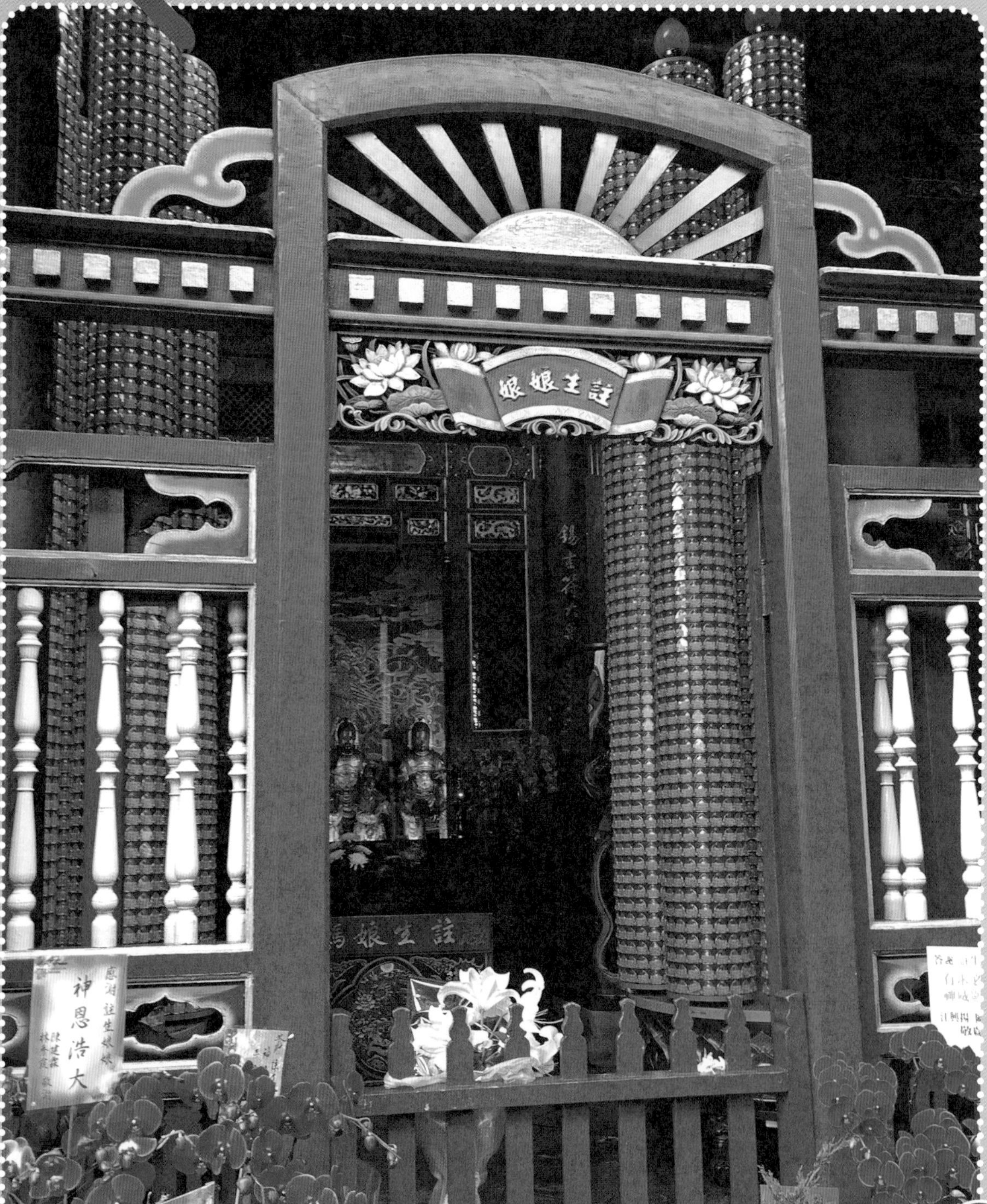

ㄅㄨˋ

【bù】

在地面下，有一顆種子，長了根，但還沒鑽出土地，意思是還沒成長的「胚」。後來這個字變成「不」的意思。當中國人同意的時候，說「好」，不同意的時候，說「不好」。

Underground, there is a seed which has roots but has not sprouted yet. This represents an embryo, something not yet mature. Over time, this character evolved to become「不」, which simply means "not." When you disagree with someone or say that something is "not good," you can write「不好」.

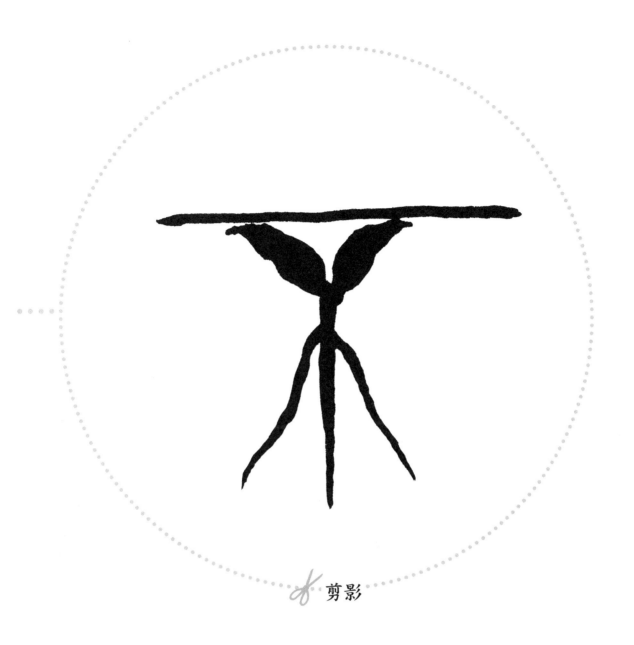

剪影

甲骨文　　金文　　小篆　　隸書　　行書　　楷體

ㄓㄨㄥ

【zhōng】

　　這個常見到的字，是「中間」的「中」。在一個長方形的物體間，不左不右地畫一直豎，就是中。

　　中也有不大不小的意思，譬如把東西分為三等，是「大中小」，一本書分為三冊，是「上中下」。

This character is one that you will see very often. A line running through the middle of a rectangle is「中」, meaning exactly what it shows – the "middle."

「中」can also mean "medium." For example, if something were classified into three sizes, it would be labelled「大、中、小」(large, medium, small). If a book were published as three volumes, they would be labelled「上、中、下」, where「中」would be the second or middle volume.

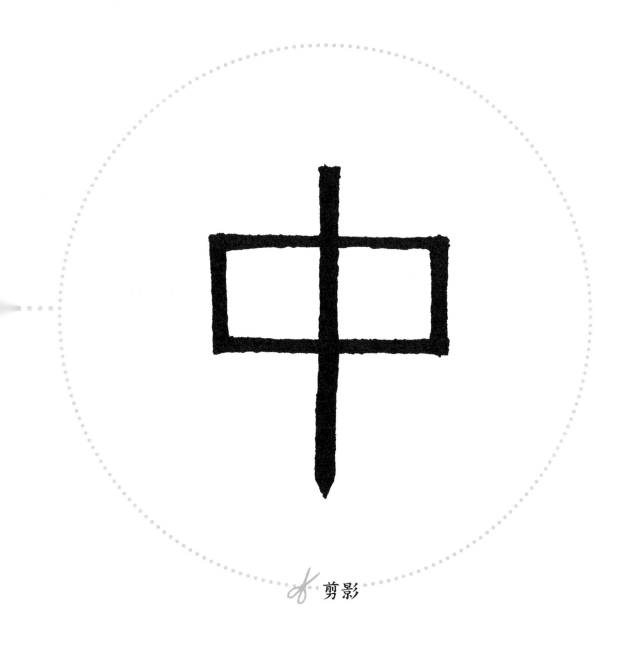

剪影

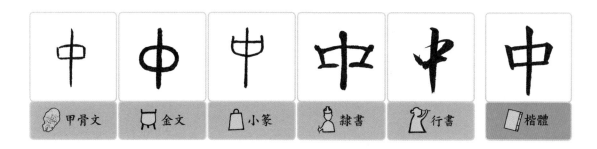

| 甲骨文 | 金文 | 小篆 | 隸書 | 行書 | 楷體 |
|---|---|---|---|---|---|

多少興亡玄秘事

盡藏深宮不言中

ㄏㄨㄚˊ

【huá】

　　「華」也是「花」，最早的「華」字就像一棵樹上開滿了花。中國人自稱「中華」，意思是在世界的中心，文化燦爛的國家。

　　「華」used to be the same character as「花」, which means "flower." The earliest form of this character looked like a flowering tree. The Chinese refer to themselves as「中華」, which means "those who thrive in the middle of the world."

剪影

| 甲骨文 | 金文 | 小篆 | 隸書 | 行書 | 楷體 |

一、

【yì】

　　「藝」像是一個人跪在地上種花。

　　中國話「手藝」的意思是專業的技術。「藝術」則專指那些有美感和創意的技術。音樂、繪畫、雕塑、文學、電影,都是藝術。

　　「藝」depicts a person kneeling on the ground, planting flowers. It means "skill" or "art." When used as 「手藝」, its meaning is "craft" or "professional skill." When used as 「藝術」, it represents the aesthetic arts: music, painting, sculpture, literature, film, etc.

剪影

| 甲骨文 | 金文 | 小篆 | 隸書 | 行書 | 楷體 |
|---|---|---|---|---|---|

捷運
藝開罐

Metro Taipei
捷運，藝術就在身邊

ㄇㄟˇ

【měi】

中國人也稱「藝術」為「美術」。

「美」是象形字，好像一個人頭上戴著羽毛或獸角的裝飾，看來很美。

但是也有人說，美這個字，是由上面的「羊」和下面的「大」合在一起變成的，意思是大大的羊很美。

「藝術」can also be called「美術」.「美」is the word for "beautiful." Its pictograph depicts a person wearing an ornate headdress, which is considered very beautiful. Some others interpret the origin of「美」differently: they say that the character is made up of「羊」(sheep) and「大」(big), thus meaning "a large sheep is very beautiful."

剪影

| 甲骨文 | 金文 | 小篆 | 隸書 | 行書 | 楷體 |

一起找一找

美：攝於臺北。

一尢ˊ

【yáng】

　　現在就讓我們看看「羊」這個字。「羊」也是象形字，就像一隻大角羊的頭。

Let's take a look at the character「羊」. It means "sheep" or "ram"; don't you think the pictograph looks like a ram's head?

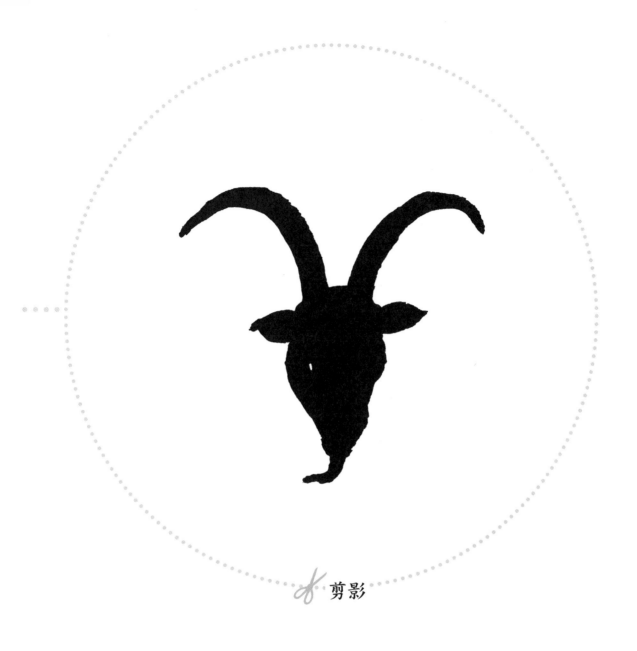

剪影

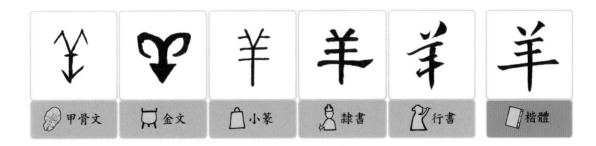

甲骨文　金文　小篆　隸書　行書　楷體

# 豬

ㄓㄨ

【zhū】

　　「豕」就是豬。早期的寫法沒有右邊的「者」，寫成「🐖」，就像一隻肚子大大、耳朵大大、腿短短、尾巴細細、鼻子長長的豬。

　　This is「豬」, which means "pig." The earliest form of this character had no「者」on the right. Its original pictograph「🐖」resembles a pot-bellied, short-legged pig with a thin tail, long snout, and big ears.

剪影

甲骨文　金文　小篆　隸書　行書　楷體

豬：攝於臺北。

ㄑㄩㄢˇ

【quǎn】

　　犬的象形字有點像「豕」，但是嘴巴特別大，尾巴也比「」長，還有尖尖大大的耳朵和爪子。

　　顯然中國人很早就養狗了，所以跟犬有關的字很多。

The original pictograph of 「犬」(meaning "dog") has many similarities to 「」, but the dog's mouth is much larger, the tail is longer and there are also pointy ears and claws. The Chinese probably domesticated dogs very early on so there are many characters with 「犬」in them.

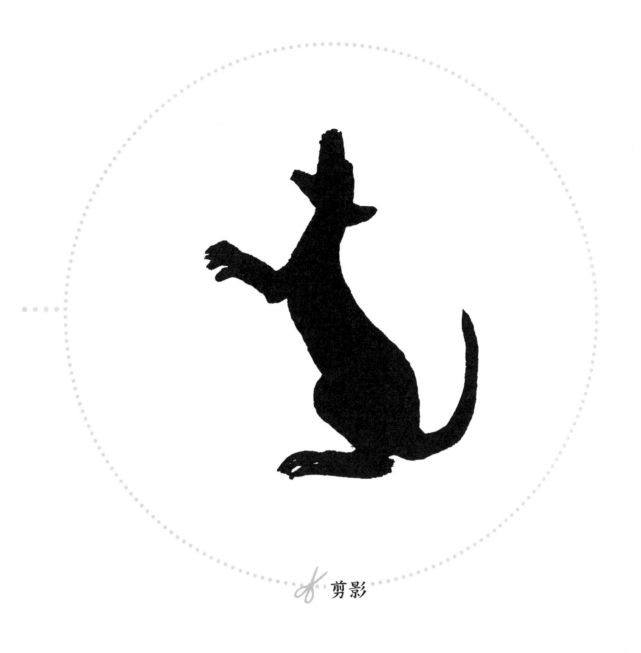

剪影

甲骨文　　金文　　小篆　　隸書　　行書　　楷體

一起找一找

犬：攝於臺北。

ㄋㄧㄠˇ

【niǎo】

　　「鳥」一看就知道是個象形字，有尖尖的喙、張開的翅膀和下面的爪子。

　　The pictograph for「鳥」is fairly obvious. See the pointy beak, spread wings, and claws.「鳥」is the word for "bird."

剪影

甲骨文　金文　小篆　隸書　行書　楷體

鳥 一起找一找
. . . . . . . . . . . . .
鳥：攝於臺北。

維護環境生態
請勿餵食鳥類
No Feeding the Birds

ㄓㄨㄟ

【zhuī】

　　「隹」也是象形字，就像一隻鳥。在中文字裡多半當「偏旁」使用，凡是有這個「隹」作邊的，常常跟鳥有關。

　　「隹」is also a pictograph that looks like a bird. It is mostly used as a part of other characters which have meanings related to birds.

剪影

| 甲骨文 | 金文 | 小篆 | 隸書 | 行書 | 楷體 |

隻

【zhī】

　　手上抓了一隻鳥，就是「隻」。大概古時候人們常彼此問「抓到幾隻鳥啊？」，被問的人就舉起手上的鳥。現在「隻」這個字多半當作「單位詞」，譬如「三隻鳥」。

Holding a bird in your hand is the pictograph of「隻」. Perhaps this started because in ancient times, people would ask each other, "How many birds did you catch today?" The hunter would then hold up the birds in his hand. Today,「隻」is a unit-measuring word, for example,「三隻鳥」would mean "three birds."

剪影

| 甲骨文 | 金文 | 小篆 | 隸書 | 行書 | 楷體 |

ㄕㄨㄤ

【shuāng】

　　手上站了兩隻鳥，意思是「雙」。中國人很喜歡這個字，常說「好事成雙」。看這個字，想想，當一個人秀給朋友看：「瞧！我手上有一對鳥。」是不是很得意？

Two birds standing on a hand symbolize the character that means "double." Chinese people like this word and often use a phrase that translates to "good things come in pairs" (or "one good thing is followed by another"). Imagine a person showing his friends: "Look! There is a pair of birds in my hand!" That's something to be proud of!

剪影

| 甲骨文 | 金文 | 小篆 | 隸書 | 行書 | 楷體 |
|---|---|---|---|---|---|
| | | 雙 | 雙 | 雙 | 雙 |

ㄒㄩㄝˊ

【xué】

　　一雙手在上面，好像結網的樣子，下面有間房子，裡面有個小孩。你可以想那是教屋裡的孩子結網的技術。這個字是「學」，可以當動詞說「學習」，也可以當名詞稱「學校」。只要在前面加上「小」、「中」或「大」，就成了小學、中學和大學。

A pair of hands on top appear to be weaving; a house at the bottom appears to contain a child. One could interpret this as teaching a child the skills of weaving. This word is 「學」, which can be used as a verb in 「學習」 (to learn) or as a noun in 「學校」 (school). Preceding it with 「小」, 「中」, or 「大」 would create the words meaning elementary school (小學), middle school (中學), and college (大學).

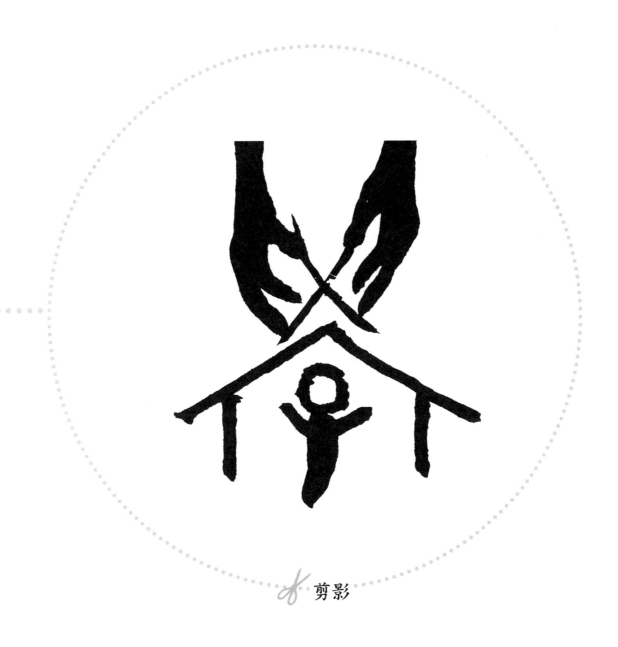

剪影

甲骨文　金文　小篆　隸書　行書　楷體

一起找一找

學：攝於臺北。

ㄩˊ

【yú】

這是個很明顯的象形字，大概連三歲的小朋友也可以看得出來是「魚」。

This is a pictograph depicting a "fish", even small children can recognize it.

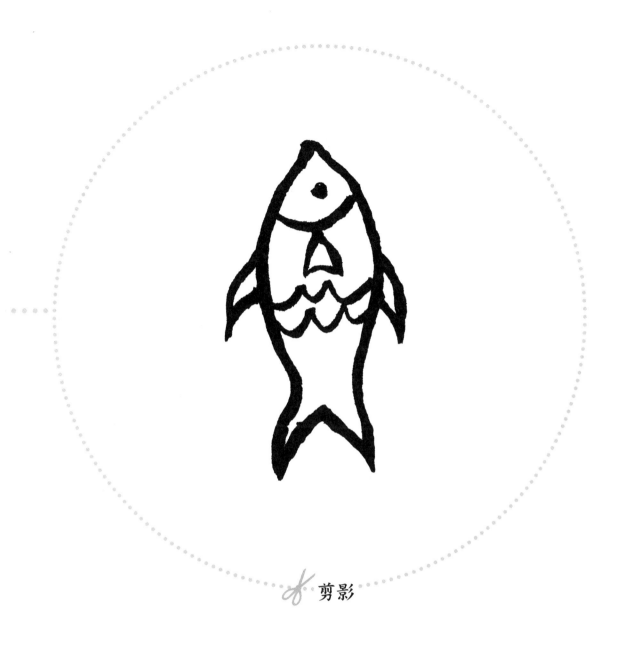

剪影

甲骨文　金文　小篆　隸書　行書　楷體

ㄍㄨㄥˋ

【gòng】

　　中間一口鍋（或一個東西），兩邊各伸出一隻手，表示二人共用、共有。這個字在中國很常用，譬如「中共」，「中」表示中國，「共」表示共產黨。

A pot（or some other object）in the center with a hand reaching towards it from either side, shows two people sharing. This word is very common in Chinese. For example,「中共」is made up of「中」(short for China) and「共」(short for the Communist Party).

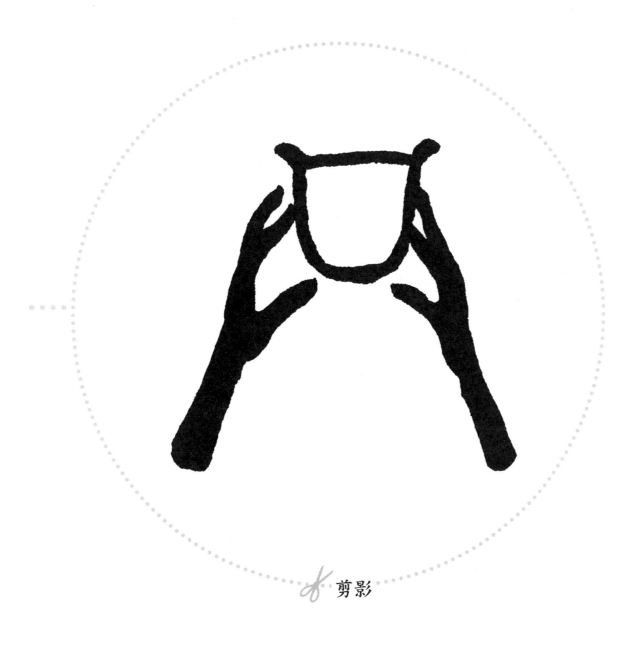

剪影

甲骨文　金文　小篆　隸書　行書　楷體

ㄆㄧㄥˊ

【píng】

　　平是平穩，不平會搖擺、會倒掉。所以平這個字像「天平」，左右平均、合於水準。今天的平字，比古人寫的還平。「平平的、穩穩的」，如果下面再加個安字，是「平安」，也是中文最常用的問候語。

　　「平」is steady, it does not shake or tip over. Therefore, the character looks like a scale, symmetrical and standard. The modern character is actually even more "balanced" and "level" than the ancient version. Adding "a woman in a house" forms「平安」, meaning safe and sound; the phrase is often also used as a greeting.

剪影

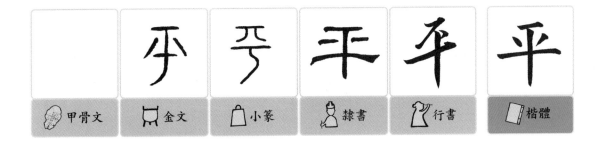

| 甲骨文 | 金文 | 小篆 | 隸書 | 行書 | 楷體 |

ㄏㄜˊ

【hé】

　　一株禾科植物，上面的穀子成熟了，彎彎地垂下來，旁邊有一張嘴。多好哇！有糧食吃了！這個字在中文裡常用。「和」加上公平的「平」，是「和平」；「和」加上揹著孩子的女人，是「和好」。

The grain is ready to be harvested and the wheat plant dips. Next to it is a mouth because there is food to eat! This word is often used in combination. For example,「和平」means peace, while「和好」means "to make peace between people."

剪影

| | 和 | 䂴 | 和 | 和 | 和 |
|---|---|---|---|---|---|
| 甲骨文 | 金文 | 小篆 | 隸書 | 行書 | 楷體 |

## ⊙ 漢字是怎麼演進的

The evolution of Hanzi Characters

# 甲骨文

中國人的老祖先很迷信，碰上重要的事，像是能不能打仗、什麼時候適合種田打獵、什麼時候會下雨、甚至王后會生男孩還是女孩，都要問老天爺。

他們問的方法很特殊——先在烏龜肚皮上的那塊甲殼或其他野獸的骨頭上鑽小孔，再把一小塊燒紅的炭或金屬放在那小洞上，甲骨被烤焦而且膨脹造成裂紋，那些巫師則根據裂紋的樣子解說老天爺給的答案，再把答案刻在裂紋的旁邊。

這些由西元前一千多年留存到今天的甲骨文上的文字，可以說是中國最早的文字。

由於甲骨文是用金屬刀子刻在很硬的甲骨上，所以多半線條很細、筆觸很直、頭尾比較尖。又因為當時的文字還沒統一，所以同一個字可能刻得不同，而且許多像圖畫，比較容易猜出它的意思。

我們由這些最早的甲骨文開始，一點一點看它們後來的演變，就好像先找到山裡的小溪，再順著往下，很容易就能找到大河，也很輕鬆地就能學會現在的漢字了。

書裡凡是作「」這個好像「烏龜肚皮甲」符號的都是甲骨文。

# Oracle Bone and Tortoise Shell Inscriptions

Shang Dynasty (c. 16th -11th century B.C.)

The ancient people of China were very superstitious. When faced with any important issue, such as whether or not the country should go to war, when it would be most suitable to farm or to hunt, how long it would be until the next rainfall, or even whether the queen would give birth to a boy or a girl, the Chinese consulted the gods.

Their method of divination involved first puncturing the interior side of tortoise shells or the bones of other animals. When a small piece of red-hot coal or metal was placed over the holes, the burnt shells or bones expanded, resulting in cracks. The oracle then interpreted the cracks as heaven's response and carved the explanation next to the cracks.

Such oracle inscriptions were produced with metal blades on hard surfaces, most of the strokes were extremely fine and straight with pointed ends. Without a unified writing system, one word could have been carved in many different ways, most of which looked like pictures.

We begin from these ancient oracle inscriptions to see how characters gradually evolved. Just like finding a small mountain stream, following its path, and coming upon a great river, we will easily learn and understand modern-day Chinese characters.

In this book, oracle inscriptions will be indicated by " " (tortoise shell symbol) .

# 金文

　　既然刻甲骨文是用刀，表示中國人早已使用金屬工具。考古學家也確實挖掘到不少當時以金屬（主要是青銅）製造的武器和餐具。其中的餐具尤其講究，像是煮食物的「鼎」、盛東西的「盤」、裝酒的「壺」，上面不但有美麗的花紋，而且常常刻鑄了文字。起初那文字很簡單，可能只像個商標圖案，漸漸愈刻愈多，甚至成為整篇大文章。

　　在銅器上刻字或鑄字，比在甲骨上麻煩得多，也自然要小心得多。所以銅器上留下來的字，多半比較整齊、筆觸較粗、分佈得較平均，也修飾得比較美。而且因為不用甲骨占卜之後，中國人還不斷製造青銅器，所以上面的金文，呈現了許多比甲骨文晚期的字。

　　書中凡是作「鼎」狀「 ∐ 」符號的，都是金文。

## Bronzeware Inscriptions

The production of oracle inscriptions by a sharp knife reveals that the Chinese had already started using metal tools. Archaeologists excavated numerous metal, especially bronze, weapons and cooking utensils. The utensils were particularly intricate; there were three-legged cooking vessels, plates, and wine bottles with beautiful embellishments and often even inscriptions. At first, those characters were simply symbols; the words gradually increased and became sentences and paragrephs.

Inscribing on bronze is much more difficult than carving into bones or tortoise shells, and required more precision. Therefore, bronzeware inscriptions are usually neater and laid out more evenly with thicker strokes and more elaborate ornaments. While the practice of bone and tortoise shell divination came to an end, the Chinese people continued to produce bronzeware. Because of this, bronzeware inscriptions display Chinese characters of a later period than oracle inscriptions.

# 小篆

　　西元前二二一年，秦始皇統一中國，他除了規定全國度量衡和車輪的距離，而且命令宰相李斯把原先寫法不同的文字標準化，是為「小篆」，至於未統一之前的文字則稱為「大篆」。兩百年後，東漢的許慎又寫了一本《說文解字》，把小篆的源流做出分析。

　　在這本書裡凡標示秤砣符號「　」的都是根據《說文解字》寫的「小篆」，可以看得出來，對比之前的大篆，每個字都成為更整齊的方塊字，筆觸也更均勻了，漢字到了這個時候已經稱得上相當進步。

## Small Seal Script

In 221 B.C., China came under the rule of its first emperor, Qin Shi Huang. In order to unify his empire, he developed a network of roads and standardized the axles of carts. Most importantly, he ordered Prime Minister Li Si to systematize Qin script by removing its variant forms, thereby creating an official set of Chinese characters, which was later called small seal script. Writing from before the standardization is known as large seal script.

After 200 years, Xu Shen of the Eastern Han Dynasty wrote *Shuowen Jiezi*, a dictionary which analyzed the origin and meaning of every small seal script character.

In this book, I use the symbol of a weight "　" to signify all excerpts from *Shuowen Jiezi*. One can see that small seal script is more orderly than oracle inscriptions and bronzeware inscriptions. Most of the words appear rectangular with more uniform brush strokes; these are already very advanced Chinese characters.

# 竹木簡牘書

　　研究中國文字，不能不瞭解中國人的毛筆。因為必須有很好用的毛筆，中國書法才能發展得那麼變化多端。

　　從史前陶器上的花紋和甲骨上寫的字，可以知道那時候已經有了不錯的毛筆。甲骨文不是刻的嗎？為什麼還有毛筆寫的痕跡呢？那是因為當時的人常先用黑墨或朱紅色的顏料寫一遍，再刻。有些字寫好了沒刻，所以現在能看到。

　　由銅器上的文字筆觸，也可以看出古人多半先用毛筆寫好刻好再鑄。可惜既然作成銅器，就再也看不到原來的筆跡了。

　　現在的人，如果想看中國人老祖先的筆跡，最好的材料是西元前五世紀左右留下的，寫在木簡和竹簡上的文字。而且因為那些字都只有寫，不必刻，有些只是帳冊、書信甚至日記，所以寫得特別自由，可以看出很多瀟灑而有個性的表現，也逐漸把中國文字從拘謹的篆體中解放出來。

　　當時中國人把一根根長長的竹片或木片用繩子編在一起。中文一直用到今天的「冊」字，就是「兩條竹木簡中間串一根繩子」的「象形字」。傳說「孔子讀易，韋編三絕」，也表示孔子當時讀的是用皮繩子編的竹簡或木簡。

# Wood and Bamboo Slip Inscriptions

To truly know Chinese characters, one must understand the Chinese brush. Chinese calligraphy could only develop so much variation with such a writing utensil.

Designs on ancient pottery and oracle inscriptions on bones are evidence of an already quite advanced brush at that time. You may be wondering, weren't oracle inscriptions carved? Then why are there still traces of a brush? That is because people often first used black ink or red pigment to write the characters as a guide for engraving. Some words were written but not carved and thus can now be seen.

From the brush stokes apparent in characters on bronze, one can see that they were usually first written with a brush and then carved. However, only bronze objects, and not their molds, have been preserved; we will never be able to actually see the original writing technique.

If people today wish to observe the handwriting of their ancestors, the best subjects would be the characters written on wood, bamboo slips, and silk (c. 5th century B.C.). Because they were only written and not engraved, they were composed freely, often in the form of account books, letters, and diaries. They were natural and individualistic expressions that helped to release Chinese language from the rigid seal script.

The Chinese word 「冊」, which still means "volume (of a book)", is a pictograph of a string going through the middle of two bamboo slips.

There is a story about Confucius reading The Book of Changes so much that the leather straps broke three times, which also implies that he studied from volumes of wood and bamboo slips.

# 隸書

　　教育愈來愈進步、知識愈來愈豐富、書信愈來愈普遍，加上西元前一世紀左右有了紙的發明，中國人覺得篆字實在太不方便了，因為既要在轉彎的地方畫得圓，又得把線條寫得勻，非常花時間。於是開始改變，筆觸向兩邊伸長而且擺動的「隸書」就出現了。如果形容寫篆字，是把雙手綁起來跳舞，「隸書」則是鬆了綁，你可以很容易地看出來寫字的人自由多了——本來圓形的框子，現在成為方形，尤其向左右的「撇」和「捺」，先壓一下，再挑起來，十分瀟灑。

　　中文「隸書」的「隸」，意思是「在下面乖乖聽話做事的人」，也可以解釋為低層公務員，因為隸書是下面辦事人員圖方便和快速最先使用的字體。為了書寫方便，中國文字由巫師使用的「甲骨文」、貴族使用的「金文」，秦始皇統一的「小篆」到漢代的「隸書」，真是愈來愈實用而且平民化了。

　　書裡凡是作「」這種「文書人員寫字」圖案的都是隸書。

# Clerical Script

With improving education, increasing knowledge, wide use of written messages and the invention of paper around 1st century B.C., the Chinese people were starting to feel the inconvenience of Small Seal Script, which was extremely time consuming to write because of its rounded edges and identical strokes. The extended and flexible brush strokes of clerical script therefore developed. Writing clerical script is like dancing with hands unbound. The formerly round frame is now rectangular; the ends of strokes involve slightly pressing down and then raising the brush, all in a carefree manner.

Because this script made record keeping quick and easy, and was used by government clerics, it is thus known as "clerical script." As we can see, the evolution of characters have moved towards convenience and accessibility. Originally only used by oracles, then by royals (bronzeware inscription), then standardized (small seal script), and used widely by clerics in the Han Dynasty, writing became more practical and familiar to daily life.

In this book, I will use " " (office worker) to symbolize clerical script.

# 行書・草書

　　如果說「篆書」是坐、「隸書」是走、「行書」應該是跑，「草書」則是飛。

　　雖然「隸書」寫起來已經比「篆書」快，為了實用，人們還是不滿意，他們要寫得更快，於是有了「行書」和「草書」。我們很難說行書和草書產生在什麼時候，因為就算早在西元前三世紀還是以小篆為主的秦代，如果打仗時軍情緊急，為了求快，也會寫行書和草書。但是至少可以說：到西元四世紀的王羲之、王獻之父子，行草已經發展到巔峰。

　　行書和草書最大的特色是它們轉動得比隸書圓滑。為了求快，寫字的人不再費時間慢慢表現每一筆的開頭和收尾，而是上一筆連著下一筆寫，就算不真的相連，每一筆之間也好像有一根無形的線牽著。「行書」比「隸書」寫得快，但比「飛快」的「草書」還慢些。所以行書筆觸連得少，不像草書有時候好幾個字不但筆筆相連，而且字字相連，好像拉起其中一根線，所有的字都能被扯起來了。

　　因為中國文人特別愛寫行書，以前又流行在牆壁上題詩，所以書中凡是有「文人在牆上題字」「🚶」符號的，都是行書或草書。

# Semi-cursive and Cursive Script

If characters had movement, then seal script would be like sitting; clerical script would be like walking, semi-cursive script would be like running, and cursive script would be like flying!

Although clerical script was already much more convenient than small seal script, people wanted to write faster, and developed semi-cursive and cursive script. It is hard to say exactly when these scripts were created because even when small seal script was officially used during the Qin Dynasty, military messages required such speed that they were often written in semi-cursive and cursive script. At the very least, one can say that both these scripts were developed to their fullest extent by the 4th century, as evident in the calligraphy of father and son Wang Xi Zhi and Wang Xian Zhi.

The greatest characteristic of semi-cursive and cursive script is the smooth motion. Writers no longer stop at the beginning and end of every stroke. Instead, each stroke follows the previous; even if they do not actually connect, they seem to be attached by an invisible line. This is especially apparent in cursive script, where not only strokes but often even multiple characters are joined, as if pulling the end of one line would raise the entire sentence off the page.

Because Chinese scholars preferred to use semi-cursive script and also because writing poems on walls used to be popular, " " will signify semi-cursive or cursive script in the book.

# 楷書

楷書又叫「真書」或「正書」，是從西元七世紀初，一直到今天中國人都使用的標準字體。除了中國大陸一九四九年之後又簡化了其中一些字，成為所謂「簡體字」，至今臺灣、香港都還在使用「楷書」，並且為了與簡體字區別，稱它為「正體字」或「繁體中文字」。

楷書應該是與行書、草書同時發展出來的，也可以說為了寫得快，並且使上一筆與下一筆更容易連接，楷書是在隸書的基礎上，加了行書和草書的一些筆觸。舉例說：小篆的「手」字邊是「」，隸書的「手」字邊是「」，草書的「手」字邊寫成「」，楷書的「手」字邊則成為「」。

比起較死板的小篆和沉重的隸書，楷書增加了許多輕巧、像小鳥啄食的「點子」和「勾」、「挑」，這些筆觸因為都是「重重落筆、輕輕出筆」，一頭鈍、一頭尖，所以寫來快些，看來也輕巧些。雖不像草書可以好幾筆相連那麼快，但是比起篆、隸，它是既工整又比較好寫的字體。從七世紀以來，中國人凡是重要的公文，絕大多數使用楷書。

這本書裡凡作「線裝書」符號「」的，都是楷書。

# Regular Script

Regular script, also known as true script and standard script, is the Chinese calligraphy style that has been used from the early 7th century to modern times. After 1949, the People's Republic of China simplified some characters, however, Taiwan and Hong Kong still use Regular Script, which is now called Traditional Chinese.

Regular script developed during approximately the same time as semi-cursive and cursive script. To write faster with better connected strokes, regular script has some cursive characteristics and the basis of clerical script. For example, the radical that means hand is 「⼿」 in small seal script, 「⼿」 in clerical script, 「⼿」 in cursive script, and 「⼿」 in regular script.

Compared to the rigid small seal script and the heavy clerical script, regular script has many light, dots, hooks, and lifts. The style is the result of landing the brush solidly and raising it gently, giving each stroke one dull end and one sharp end. Although it is not as fast to write as cursive script, it is certainly neat and efficient. Since the 7th century, the Chinese have used regular script for most official documents.

In the book, "⬜"will symbolize regular script.

# 簡體漢字

嚴格說一般所稱的「中文字」，應該叫作「漢字」，因為中國許多民族都早有自己的文字，只因為漢人佔大多數，所以採取漢字為全國通用的文字。

今天所謂的簡體漢字，除了少數是新造的，許多都在以前的行書或草書裡出現過，也可以說雖然從七世紀到二十世紀，中國人都用「楷書」，但是人們為了求快，早就發展出一些簡體字。譬如「幾」寫成「几」、「畫」寫成「画」、「舉」寫成「举」、「舊」寫成「旧」、「龜」寫成「龟」、「勸」寫成「劝」、「區」寫成「区」、「慶」寫成「庆」、「親」寫成「亲」、「橋」寫成「桥」、「豈」寫成「岂」、「盡」寫成「尽」、「擊」寫成「击」、「還」寫成「还」、「蝦」寫成「虾」、「開」寫成「开」、「會」寫成「会」、「國」寫成「国」、「龍」寫成「龙」、「劉」寫成「刘」、「麗」寫成「丽」、「歷」寫成「历」、「難」寫成「难」、「頭」寫成「头」、「廳」寫成「厅」、「達」寫成「达」、「當」寫成「当」、「豐」寫成「丰」、「無」寫成「无」、「寶」寫成「宝」。以上這些字，就算完全不懂中文的人也可以看得出「後者」好寫得多。

此外在「偏旁」上，中國大陸也是根據行書和草書簡化。譬如「言」字邊寫成「讠」，「食」字邊寫成「饣」，「車」字邊寫成「车」。由此可知學習四世紀的行書和草書，對認識今天的「簡體漢字」也有幫助。漢字怎麼變，還是血脈相通的。

# Simplified Chinese

Technically, what we now call "Chinese characters" should be called "Han characters." The numerous tribes of ancient China all had their own language; because Han had the largest population, Han characters were chosen to be China's official writing system.

Except for those that were newly created, the majority of modern simplified Chinese characters had appeared in semi-cursive or cursive script. Even though regular script was used from the 7th to the 21st century, people developed some simplified characters for speed. Examples are shown in the table below. Obviously, the simplified characters are easier to write.

Much of this simplification is actually based on semi-cursive and cursive script. For example, "言" (speech) is written as "讠", "食" (food) as "饣", "車" (car) as "车". Learning about the semi-cursive and cursive script of the 4th century can thus help us to better appreciate modern-day simplified Chinese. Regardless of how much Chinese characters change, they are all still related by lineage.

| 楷書<br>Regular Script | 幾 | 畫 | 舉 | 舊 | 龜 | 勸 | 區 | 慶 | 親 | 橋 |
|---|---|---|---|---|---|---|---|---|---|---|
| 簡體漢字<br>Simplified Chinese | 几 | 画 | 举 | 旧 | 龟 | 劝 | 区 | 庆 | 亲 | 桥 |

| 楷書<br>Regular Script | 豈 | 盡 | 擊 | 還 | 蝦 | 開 | 會 | 國 | 龍 | 劉 |
|---|---|---|---|---|---|---|---|---|---|---|
| 簡體漢字<br>Simplified Chinese | 岂 | 尽 | 击 | 还 | 虾 | 开 | 会 | 国 | 龙 | 刘 |

| 楷書<br>Regular Script | 麗 | 難 | 頭 | 廳 | 達 | 當 | 豐 | 無 | 寶 |
|---|---|---|---|---|---|---|---|---|---|
| 簡體漢字<br>Simplified Chinese | 丽 | 难 | 头 | 厅 | 达 | 当 | 丰 | 无 | 宝 |

## ⊙ 作者簡介
About the Authors

### 劉墉 Yung Liu

聞名兩岸的畫家、作家、教育家。出版文學藝術作品一百餘種，被譯為英韓泰越等國文字，在世界各地個展三十餘次。

One of the most influential and popular writers of the Chinese speaking world, and also a renowned painter and educator, Mr. Liu has written over one hundred books of essays, prose, short fiction, inspiration literature and art analysis, and his books have been translated to English, Korean, Thai and many other international editions. As a painter, Mr. Liu has held more than thirty solo exhibitions throughout the world, and his artworks are regularly featured in Sotheby's, Christie's and other major auction houses.

## 劉軒 Xuan Liu

音樂家、作家、演說家及主持人，美國哈佛大學心理學碩士及博士研究，出版中英韓文作品十餘種。

Musician, writer, speaker, radio show host. Holds BA from Harvard University and M.Ed from the Harvard Graduate School of Education. He is also a classically trained pianist and one of the most in-demand DJs in Taiwan. As a writer, he has written eleven books and translated several other works.

## 劉倚帆 Yvonne Liu

美國哥倫比亞大學畢業，賓州大學華頓商學院研究生。曾任美國華納兄弟娛樂公司中國區經理，出版英文翻譯作品兩種。

Graduate of Columbia University and current MBA candidate at The Wharton School of the University of Pennsylvania. Former Manager of China for Warner Bros. Entertainment Inc. She has previously translated two books from Chinese to English.

• 三位作者已經將本書在台首版版稅全數捐給台灣公益團體。細目見水雲齋官網（syzstudio.com）
The author and translators have generously donated all royalties from the first printing to social and charitable causes.

# 索引

**聯合文叢 605**

## 漢字有意思！
### 跟著劉墉一家趣味玩漢字

作　　　者／劉墉◎中文‧圖；劉軒、劉倚帆◎英文翻譯
發 行 人／張寶琴

總 編 輯／李進文
責 任 編 輯／黃榮慶
專 案 編 輯／陳惠珍
專 案 設 計／BEAR
資 深 美 編／戴榮芝
校　　　對／劉墉　劉軒　黃榮慶　陳惠珍　李進文
業務部總經理／李文吉
財 務 部／趙玉瑩　韋秀英
人事行政組／李懷瑩
版 權 管 理／黃榮慶
法 律 顧 問／理律法律事務所
　　　　　　陳長文律師、蔣大中律師

出 版 者／聯合文學出版社股份有限公司
地　　　址／（110）臺北市基隆路一段 178 號 10 樓
電　　　話／（02）27666759 轉 5107
傳　　　真／（02）27567914
郵 撥 帳 號／17623526 聯合文學出版社股份有限公司
登 記 證／行政院新聞局版臺業字第 6109 號
網　　　址／http://unitas.udngroup.com.tw
　　　　　　E-mail:unitas@udngroup.com.tw

印 刷 廠／瑞豐實業股份有限公司
總 經 銷／聯合發行股份有限公司
地　　　址／（231）新北市新店區寶橋路 235 巷 6 弄 6 號 2 樓
電　　　話／（02）29178022

版權所有‧翻版必究
出 版 日 期／2016 年 8 月　　　初版
　　　　　　2016 年 12 月 23 日　初版十三刷
定　　　價／360 元

ISBN 978-986-323-172-1（軟精裝）
《本書如有缺頁、破損、裝幀錯誤、請寄回調換》